Further Praise for
Management Lessons from the E.R.

"Paul's the Man. I love the analogies between saving a life and saving a business. I'd entrust Paul with both. Every business should have a Paul on call."

— Guy Kawasaki, CEO, Garage Technology Ventures, and Author,

"Truly refreshing! Dr. Auerbach has taken icine and business, added common sense ence, and produced an entertaining bu managers."

— Sam Colella, Managing Director, Versant Ventures

"Drawing upon his vast experience as a physician and businessman, Dr. Auerbach shares many fascinating and instructive 'prescriptions for success' that will help today's business leaders to diagnose and treat their business problems. Having practiced decision making in life-or-death situations in the emergency room, Auerbach offers his insights and insightful rules for treating the unexpected daily crises and problems of the business world."

— H. Robert Heller, Executive Vice President and Director,
Fair Isaac and Co., Inc.

"Dr. Auerbach converts years of medical intelligence and experience into practical wisdom for leaders. He clarifies nuances of human motivation and behavior and unveils the real dynamics of effective organizations. Written with wit, insight, and compassion, his style is riveting. Like the grand finale of E.R., this work moves at multiple levels—the crisis that teaches, the relationships that hold us, and the human drive to achieve because it is the right thing to do—and demonstrates the value of careful observation, appropriate response to crisis, and telling the truth."

— David J. Nygren, Ph.D., Consultant, William M. Mercer, Inc.

"Corporate and organizational leaders face unprecedented challenges, and the need to learn from cross-industry experience has never been greater. In this provocative and instructive book, Dr. Auerbach marries his insights as a physician and businessman to espouse a refreshing approach to management. You're bound to be stimulated by his candid and creative perspective!"

— Kenneth W. Kizer, M.D., M.P.H., President and CEO,
The National Quality Forum

"Dr. Auerbach's colorful analogies between managing a business and managing patients in the emergency room bring to life the challenges of running a company in a compelling and easily understood fashion. This is not another boring business book filled with long lists of outdated rules. As he does with the comatose patients who enter his emergency room, Auerbach has brought the subject matter to life!"

— Patrick Latterell, Partner, Venrock Associates

"Auerbach offers a one-of-a-kind perspective to business managers. On both money and medicine, the book is as informative as a textbook, yet it is as fun to read as a novel—no, that's an understatement—it's as fun to read as watching an episode of E.R. If I had trouble with my body or my business, I'd consult Auerbach."

— Timothy J. Groseclose, Associate Professor of Political Economics,
Stanford Graduate School of Business

"The principles of the book are easy to understand and just as easy to apply. 'When you circle the wagons, don't shoot in' is one of my favorite Auerbach analogies. I have already used it a number of times to help teams from different companies work together toward the development of a multi-million-dollar project."

— Sandra Holloway, Vice President, SAIC

"Dr. Auerbach presents a sensible, thoughtful guide to running a business and managing all of the challenges attendant therein. His many years of experience handling medical emergencies, dealing thoughtfully, expediently, and respectfully with patients, and teaching these skills to others, combined with his many years of business experience, offer the reader a uniquely sage wisdom. This is not your standard business theory book, but an engaging invitation to rethink management strategy. Dr. Auerbach's advice is not only valuable in the workplace, but also in daily living."

— Michael Tucker, President, Books, Inc.

"Paul Auerbach has captured the clarity of purpose for business that emergency medicine by necessity requires. This book effectively underscores the critical business factors faced by every CEO. It's a great prescription for any company's health!"

—Barbara Cannon, CEO, Celeris Corporation

"A great concept! Auerbach infuses key business concepts with the clear thinking and humanity of good medicine. The fascinating stories of a busy emergency room allow an objective look at the troubling realities of managing in today's business climate. A clear, concise, and enjoyable read that will serve both the business novice as well as the more experienced executive."

— David Kaplan, M.D., Principal, Tillinghast Towers Perrin

"I think the analogy of a business as a living organism, with lots of variables and interrelated systems, is right on. Auerbach's plan to extend this further by identifying symptoms, diagnoses, and treatments will be extremely helpful to any manager. The fact that the Hippocratic compassion is evident in his philosophy is welcome in today's world, where top managers who are autocratic seem to promote that fact endlessly, but those who motivate with a combination of the carrot and the stick are more successful in the long run. And that, in the end, is the true win. I think Auerbach is talking to an audience that is focused on quarterly earnings reports and telling them that they are actually engaged in a longer-term process to create a sustainable system. The good news is that his treatment includes *many* actionable items."

— David M. Burk, President, Clear Ink

"Dr. Auerbach succinctly reflects the parallels between managing patient care in the E.R. and managing a traditional business. His use of analogies and stories highlights unique insights into modern business challenges. Experienced medical practitioners are by necessity practical, and this becomes even more important if they embark upon a career change. This is a must-read for everyone who considers interactions with people to be at the core of their business."

— Stephen J. Sullivan, M.D., Venture Partner, Skyline Ventures

"The lightbulb just turned on! I realize why Paul Auerbach is such a good doctor. When I seek a medical consultation from him, he treats me like a client, rather than a patient. He's a good manager who happens to have great medical skills. I never realized before that the successful practices of medicine and management have so much in common. Like the reading of a mystery, I found myself skipping ahead to find out the appropriate clinical decisions."

— Patricia Lee-Hoffman, Principal, Triage Consulting Group

"*Management Lessons from the E.R.* is a real-life, straightforward guide for maintaining the health of a business. This is not theory, but grounded in fundamental human values and beliefs. Dr. Auerbach's background in medicine and business uniquely qualifies him to prescribe practical approaches to the issues and challenges facing business leaders. His collection of tales bring to life lessons that would otherwise take years to learn."

— Mark Giresi, Vice President of Operations, The Limited, Inc.

"Dr. Auerbach uses his experiences in a busy university emergency medicine program to explain how some of the approaches to emergency medical care can be extrapolated to other businesses in a thoughtful—and thought provoking—way. He's able to take concrete examples from his diagnostic and clinical approach to sick patients and define creative methods for addressing financial, administrative, and organizational problems in a business. Using the tools described in this book, any manager can better evaluate the condition of a company and chart a healthy course."

— Neal H. Cohen, M.D., Vice Dean, School of Medicine, University of California, San Francisco

"As medicine in the E.R. requires continuous decision making, including triage, assessment, and intervention, so does management of a high-potential business venture. With his sharp insights and clear vision, Dr. Auerbach sheds new light on the realities of management. First-time entrepreneurs and experienced managers alike will benefit from an approach that emphasizes human factors and common sense."

— Jerome S. Engel, Executive Director, Lester Center for Entrepreneurship and Innovation, University of California at Berkeley

"Crisis can bring out the best or the worst in any manager. This book guides us through real-life lessons learned from the quintessential crisis environment of an E.R. while it teaches us what it takes to be prepared. Every manager should take advantage of this advice, particularly in the calm before the storm."

— Katherine Kim, CEO, Communications Technology Cluster, LLC

"My life has been devoted to medicine—clinical practice, discovery, and entrepreneurship. But until I read this book, I didn't recognize the logic and power of applying my profession to the greater world of business. Paul Auerbach is world famous as an emergency physician because of his teaching, and now he excels as a business leader. Cover to cover, the book is packed with important insights. As he cares for his patients and students, Auerbach cares for your business. Managers, read this book and be healed!"

— Richard S. Stack, M.D., Managing General Partner, Synecor, LLC

"This book is a wake-up call for all of us in business. The extreme sensitivity to mankind that physicians have developed over generations will need to be a key attribute for business leaders to succeed in the future."

— Gerard Moufflet, Managing Director, Advent International

"The Advisory Board's mission is to provide valuable insights and information to business leaders. We identify trends and best practices in order to guide the thinking of decision makers. Dr. Auerbach has just given us a poignant new approach to understanding organizational behavior. His thoughtful comments about management take into account the need to balance the underlying business objective with the needs of the employees who form the backbone of the enterprise. I've seen him in action, and he walks the talk."

— Frank Williams, CEO, The Advisory Board Company

"Dr. Auerbach uses his unique background as an accomplished physician and businessman to dispense highly effective prescriptions for business managers. His medicine for business goes down smoothly and should improve the health of many ventures!"

— Gil Kliman, M.D., M.B.A., General Partner, Interwest Partners

"This is an entertaining treasure trove of a doctor's common sense that translates into financial wisdom. Dr. Auerbach offers a clever synthesis of bedrock principles from the worlds of medicine and business—the *Merck Manual* meets *The Wall Street Journal*."

— Donald Dafoe, M.D., Samuel D. Gross Professor and Chairman, Department of Surgery, Thomas Jefferson Medical College

"Anyone who manages a company, whether a struggling start-up or a Fortune 100 success, works long, lonely hours and faces deep lows and exhilarating highs. Anyone who works in an emergency room learns that the first thing to do in a crisis is to take your own pulse. Very few people are intimately familiar with both situations. Dr. Auerbach has directed prestigious academic E.R.'s, advised young companies in Silicon Valley, and guided publicly traded corporations. In this very unique book, he dissects medicine and business, finds similar patterns, and uses provocative examples to challenge the conventional wisdom of management gurus. As a physician-turned-entrepreneur, I wish I had read this book years ago. A definite must-read!"

— Giovanni Colella, M.D., CEO, Healinx

"Dr. Auerbach's skill, experience, and dedication as an E.R. physician provide valuable insights for anyone faced with the complex challenges of nurturing and healing the organism known as a business. Everyone will enjoy the metaphors that are based on real medical moments, and appreciate their application to everyday issues in the corporate environment."

— Joseph Feshbach, Executive Chairman, Curative Health Services

"Most business executives would never believe they could learn anything from the way skilled doctors manage their practices, but the lessons Paul Auerbach has learned from his years in the E.R. have clear applicability to the business world. M.B.A.'s have more in common with M.D.'s than they thought."

— Craig Johnson, Chairman and Co-Founder, Venture Law Group

*f*P

Also by Paul S. Auerbach, M.D.

Medicine for the Outdoors

A Medical Guide to Hazardous Marine Life

Diving the Rainbow Reefs. *A Photographer's Adventures Underwater*

An Ocean of Colors

Bad Medicine

Wilderness Medicine

Field Guide to Wilderness Medicine

MANAGEMENT LESSONS

FROM THE

E. R.

Prescriptions for Success
in Your Business

Paul S. Auerbach, M.D.

THE FREE PRESS

NEW YORK   LONDON   TORONTO   SYDNEY   SINGAPORE

THE FREE PRESS
A Division of Simon & Schuster, Inc.
1230 Avenue of the Americas
New York, NY 10020

For more information regarding special discounts for bulk purchases,
please contact Simon & Schuster Special Sales at 1-800-456-6798
or business@simonandschuster.com

Designed by Jan Pisciotta

Manufactured in the United States of America

1 3 5 7 9 10 8 6 4 2

Library of Congress Cataloging-in-Publication Data is available.

ISBN   978-1-4516-0608-9

This book is dedicated to all persons in business
who see beyond the dollar signs and to all doctors
who strive each day to heal with integrity.

Acknowledgments

No author writes without assistance, and no doctor practices alone. I am grateful for the keen eye of Fred Hill, the business acumen of Jim Bochnowski, and the medical wisdom of the late Jim McGuire. Dominick Anfuso and Kristen McGuiness of Simon & Schuster are delightful. As they have been countless times before, my family remains patient with me as I struggle to find the balance between teaching and learning.

INTRODUCTION

"Dr. Auerbach, we need you in Room One. *Now.*"

The patient wasn't breathing. His heart had stopped beating and his skin was blue. As I grabbed the defibrillator paddles, I noticed a young observer beginning to swoon. I figured it was the first time he was this close to watching someone die. "Are you OK?" I asked while I shocked the patient and watched his torso rise from the gurney in response to the jolt.

"I think I know him," the young man whispered.

"Well, take a look." He came closer and the remaining color drained from his face. "It's my dad's partner." I was doing a venture capitalist friend a favor and allowing his son to follow me around the E.R. because he was interested in a health-care career.

"Better step outside," I told my friend's son as I administered a second shock. It was touch and go for fifteen minutes, but I restored my patient's heartbeat and whipped him upstairs for an emergency angioplasty. He was saved.

Two hours later, I walked into the Dean's office to discover a colleague who had been raked over the coals for missing his revenue number. My friend shook with anger as he mumbled profanities under his breath. He was about to lose control and worsen the situation. I had been to business school and was a seasoned veteran of the academic trenches.

"Better step outside," I told him as I began to formulate a plan for how to manage his dilemma. I crafted a strategy and calmed him down. He walked away with a deal instead of a demotion. He was saved. At the time, I was struck by how adrenaline was my hormone du jour. Being a doctor in an E.R. could be helpful in a business situation. The seed was planted.

Soon thereafter, a professor at the Stanford Business School, Gene Webb, invited me to lecture on crisis management.

"Hell, Paul," he told me, "you probably handle more crises in a week than most corporate execs see in a lifetime. What do you think?"

It was an interesting challenge. How do you convert encounters as diverse as delivering a baby in the parking lot, diagnosing an earache, and managing a heart attack into useful lessons for business managers? Can you diagnose a cancer in your company like you can a melanoma on a surfer's nose? The easy analogies popped up—Be Prepared (I showed the class a slide of a disaster communications center); Know Your Resources (slide of a search dog); Don't Panic! (slide of a man who fell off a ladder and embedded a chisel in his forehead); Place Your Best Person in Charge (slide of me in a white coat). When I spoke, the business students easily made the stretch from medicine to management. What really held their attention was the inherent *common sense* of it all. Everybody can relate to diseases and cures. *Certain truisms are universal when framed in the appropriate context.*

Soon thereafter, I left academia and became a public company COO, where this concept was constantly reinforced. I became completely convinced that the lessons I had learned in the E.R. were superbly valid preparation for my role as a business leader. I sought the best qualities needed by effective managers, and kept citing examples of behaviors I had come to admire in my life as a physician executive. Brilliant businessmen are insightful, collaborative, decisive, and honest. These also happen to be the qualities of the great doctors.

Today I divide my time between venture capital, advising senior managers in start-up companies, and treating patients in the E.R. What impresses me with each of these activities is that there can be as much excitement (and danger) in managing a company as there is in resuscitating a motorcycle accident victim. Every day, I see fascinating new parallels between the juggling act of a hectic E.R. and all the balls that someone throws into the air to run a business. I've become thoroughly persuaded that a healing approach is the right answer for much of what we encounter on the job and in our personal lives. I'm amazed by how I can apply the reflexes and skills of an "E.R. doc" to problems in the corporate environment. *I believe these observations can help you, too!* Because I'm a doctor, people see me as a problem solver. This book evolved to help business leaders become problem solvers.

✢ ✢ ✢

The management gurus preach that you are inside a tornado or bridging a chasm, that you are too trusting or too paranoid, or that you need to downsize, upsize, reorganize, proselytize, sanitize, or "something-ize." There are rules for chief executives, rules for Board members, and even rules for revolutionaries. This is often momentum stuff. I contend that in the midst of chaos, there are guiding principles, fundamentals that doctors "in the pit" figure out as soon as they face their first cardiac arrest. The best doctors and managers come to realize that there truly are constants in a relentless sea of change. What you *always* need to know and be able to implement isn't necessarily trendy. The basics *never* change. Like any other complex organism, *like yourself*, your business can be healthy or sick. The same way you need to maintain your physical and emotional health, you need to maintain your corporate health. In other words, when precious vital organs start to falter and fail, it's time to call the doctor.

We should learn from our successes and failures alike. Merely paying attention and keeping an open mind can identify most of what's important. Running a company isn't simple, but it doesn't have to be that complicated, either. Believe it or not, it's the same with saving a life. True crises never become routine, but *much of the threat and urgency can be mitigated by being as well prepared as possible.*

As you read this book, think of a doctor as a manager, and the patient as a customer. A reflective CEO should be able to see the parallels. However, I'm not going to stretch analogies between medicine and business to the point of absurdity. The life cycle of a human being is not the same as that of a company because humans (at least in the year 2002) must be newborns, infants, toddlers, children, adolescents, young adults, middle aged adults, and elders, in that specific order, before they die. In contrast, there's no biologic clock ticking to force your company to do anything in particular (although we venture capitalists might tell you that there is no such thing as a "CEO for all seasons . . .").

I hope you find this book provocative, and can use it to react smarter and more quickly. In the E.R., it's often all up to you. But remember, while the truly great healers have historically been the finest diagnosticians with incredible intuition, those doctors needed to look things up, too. Realize right now that what you already know how to do is *supposed* to take less effort—it's mastering the self-discipline required to continuously learn and improve that's difficult.

The First Prescription for Success

Doctors write prescriptions. *Consider this book to be a prescription for success in business, written by a doctor of companies.* For this purpose, it's important to distinguish between "medicine" and the "business of medicine." There's a clear difference between the art of healing and the transfer of money. This book derives its approach from the former, not the latter. It's not obsessed with economics—rather, it's about how the thought processes of a healer can be applied to the organism known as a business. The spirit in which I offer my advice is the same as the spirit in which I write a prescription for a patient. First, I try to understand what's wrong, then figure out what I can best recommend to treat the problem. The pharmacist issues the medication and a few warnings about side effects, and then everybody keeps their fingers crossed. Different people have different reactions to different drugs, but by and large, there is predictability to the method. So it is with the business "prescriptions" that follow. I have managed very effectively as a doctor and as a business leader, so I know what I'm talking about.

Take the time to understand your business and learn from others who have gone before you, so you'll be in a good position to make diagnoses and apply some excellent cures. Be creative and seek every opportunity to look for situations that lead to opportunities for your business to become the master of its own health. Approach your business with an open mind. Be patient. Observe well. Don't jump to conclusions. Take two aspirin and call me in the morning. Just kidding.

When you become a doctor, you must set an example, particularly for others who will in time have influence upon others. If you take the correct approach, you will be an apostle of wellness, not disease.

THE DOCTOR'S OFFICE

The doctor's office is where he or she practices the art of medicine. For me, it's the E.R. and comes in two parts—the clinical arena and administrative office. In your company, the same holds true. You must deal with operations out on the sales floor or in a factory, while effectively supporting the "back office" and full range of business support systems. When I see patients, my actions are always on display and subject to constant evaluation. Workers who cannot hide in an office are similarly vulnerable. As one ascends the corporate ladder, the opportunities for daily critique diminish while milestones and mathematical performance indicators become measures of success. Senior managers must learn to balance increased responsibility with essential recollections of what key outcomes are considered by customers to represent success. In this section, learn how a physician best resonates with his environment, and how you must resonate with yours.

Every Tale of Rescue Begins with a Story about How the Victim Got into Trouble

Crisis management is predicated upon having a crisis to manage. I can't begin to tell you how many times I've had a patient tell me something like, "Doc, I've been spitting up blood for months," or, "You know, I noticed a year ago that this lump on my back was getting bigger."

Nothing in medicine is more heartbreaking than yielding to a serious illness that could have been eradicated if the victim had sought early medical attention. (That goes double for doctors, who are the masters of denial.) The value of mandatory screening programs is in the recognition that laypersons are not medically sophisticated, don't always pick up on warning signs, and procrastinate when faced with personal medical problems.

It's the same in a company. *When you hear hoofbeats and look out the window, don't expect to see zebras.* In medicine, a tremendous amount of resources is consumed searching for obscure causes of routine symptoms, perhaps in the name of defensive medicine, but more likely because doctors are paradoxically trained to look past the obvious. With the exception of intentional acts of disruption, such as malicious dissemination of anthrax, that doesn't make sense. When a person has a fever and throws up, it could certainly be a rare presentation of some tropical parasite, but it's usually just some community-acquired virus. The investigation should be prudent and cost effective.

Common things being common, there are behaviors within every organization that can serve as the canaries in the coal mine. It's extremely valuable to list the most likely adverse situations that can develop in your business and to install a methodology to recognize when they occur. *The greatest flaws reside in the area of general communication, often with employees and always with customers.* Therefore, the most important general screening program in business is customer satisfaction. It's like pain—when someone hurts, it's most often a genuine expression of suffering that causes you to investigate and find the problem. Customer complaints or declining satisfaction are just like a report of pain—there's a problem buried in there—and you need to find out what it is in order to apply an appropriate remedy.

When a problem arises, look for the ordinary causes, not the obscure configurations that are more rare and difficult to unravel. If you need to perform more diagnostics, you haven't lost precious time, and if you're on the money, the crisis is solved with a minimum expenditure of effort and money. That doesn't mean your approach should be simple. Rather, it means that common things being common, most adverse events in business are predictable and easily diagnosed, and therefore should have been previously encountered.

It's impossible to know what's going wrong if you aren't keeping in touch with your business. If you delegate that responsibility down, you'd better be certain that you've chosen someone who isn't afraid to give you the bad news when it exists. You don't have to shoot the messenger too many times before he'll stop sending you messages. Under no circumstance should you be out of touch with your customers.

As a doctor, I plead with patients to have mammograms, endure sigmoidoscopies, and lower their cholesterol. If a mole changes color or your chest hurts when you exercise, see your doctor. As an executive, I plead with my employees to keep track of our revenues and expenses, meet with our key staff and customers regularly, understand what motivates the sales force, and remember that I hate surprises, unless it's a windfall quarter. I expect them to stay in touch. In return, I give them the support they need. If someone comes to me with a problem and I can't help in a professional manner that enhances independence and motivation in a respectful way, then I'm useless.

Taking feedback is very important, but can be oh, so painful. Introspection and self-criticism have a certain value, but they're much too soft. Nothing is more revealing than letting your customers and employees tell you what they think. If you set up a way to periodically endure unfiltered comments, this feedback can become the best stethoscope into the heart of your business.

"911" Only Works When Somebody Answers the Phone

Hiking in Alaskan woods, you're startled by a scream. A young woman stumbles out of the brush, pleading for assistance.

"Somebody help me. Oh dear God, somebody *help* me!"

Her shirt and pants are torn, she's bleeding buckets from a huge gash in her forehead, hysteria has overwhelmed her, and as you race to her side, she collapses. You look behind her and see a large brown bear forty yards down the trail. The feral behemoth snarls as it threatens to move closer. You instinctively reach for your mobile phone, then realize that the nearest transmitter is probably at least three hundred miles away. So much for "911."

Select the best answer:

a. Ignore the victim and climb a tree.

b. Run like hell.

c. Throw the victim over your shoulder and try to climb the tree with her.

d. Make loud noises and try to intimidate the bear.

e. Carry the victim and slowly retreat from the bear. If the bear attacks, cover the victim's body with your own, curl into a ball, tuck your head, and protect the back of your neck with your hands.

Your decision depends on how much you *really* understand about your situation—about bleeding, bears, and your personal capacity to manage fear. An emergency rescue isn't available. One of the first things you need to learn as a physician is to know your limits, to understand what you know and what you *don't know*. So, it's critically important to recognize *ahead of time* what to do in a crisis, and not count on being able to improvise in a split second during a critical event.

Let's take this analogy to the corporate suite. You're the COO. No one in your company except the senior executives is aware that the company's in danger of missing its first quarter ever. The analysts are skeptical about your sector, so you can pretty much assume that your stock price will get hammered on the news. It also happens that your independent auditors notice a discrepancy in how revenue has been booked and mention their findings to you. This is an error that should not have occurred and its timing compounds your concern. On questioning your Controller, he breaks down and tells you that he was instructed by the CFO to cook the books. Knowing that the Street will hold the entire senior management team accountable, you drop to your knees.

Select the best answer:

    a. Race to the CEO and inform him what happened. Seek his input and follow his instructions.

    b. Contact an attorney, lay it all out, and establish attorney-client privilege for your personal protection.

    c. Discuss your findings with the CFO and allow him to correct the situation if possible.

    d. Take your findings to the Board of Directors.

    e. Write a long memorandum and deliver it to the Securities and Exchange Commission just before you resign from the company.

How you react depends on the details of the transgression, how many persons are involved, what actions need to be taken to correct the misrepresentation, and whether there is a material impact upon the company and shareholders.

What's the lesson? A business manager who purports to be in control needs to be up to speed about the worst possible hazards way ahead of when they might occur. If your company is in trouble and, metaphorically, your employees collapse in your arms, do you call for help? Sure, if it's available. But the wrong time to learn where the fire extinguishers are stored is after a fire has started. Under the assumption that sooner or later someone in your company will be dishonest, you should have thought through how you would handle a serious transgression. Here are some suggestions for this particular scenario:

1. If time permits, gather all the facts. Don't overreact based on incomplete knowledge.

2. Rank the problems and deal first with the ones that require an immediate response. At the same time, take steps to prevent a reoccurrence. (When a snake bites you, don't just stand there and take the next bite—back away!) *Never trust a dishonest person when he says, "I've learned my lesson. It won't happen again."* After someone has been intentionally deceitful and you have scrambled to save your company, get rid of the troublemaker.

3. Seek early legal advice. Find an expert and
   establish your credibility as an honest problem solver.

4. If the accounting error can be rectified, do so
   promptly and with documentation of good
   intentions.

5. Try not to disintegrate the business to evict a
   few vile rodents. In all likelihood, the vast
   majority of your employees are hardworking
   and law-abiding citizens who would never
   consider a dishonest act.

6. Put fail-safe systems in place to prevent the
   problem from ever happening again. Include
   a compliance program that *any* employee can
   use to report a suspected transgression. The
   submissions should go to in-house counsel
   or someone who is above reproach and not
   afraid to confront anyone on any issue.

There's a great benefit to anticipating problems beyond
just dealing with catastrophes. It means that you really
need to understand operations, which you may choose to
manipulate to become more efficient. For instance, I know
that patients who come to the E.R. are regularly frustrated
by long waits. If I analyze the steps involved with "processing" a patient, I can predict where things will go
wrong, so I can speed everything up when the system
starts to bog down. At the same time, I now have the
knowledge to preempt the problem in the first place.

The Truth Lies Somewhere in the Middle

They'll chisel this adage on my tombstone. I've probably spoken it more than any other aphorism to move a dispute from defensive rhetoric to the beginning of a resolution. It's necessary to get people to come off biased extreme positions, or to move from excuses to resolutions.

The intern tells me, "Dr. Auerbach, I asked the patient how much she drinks a day. She told me an occasional glass of wine, that she never gets drunk. Her abdomen was soft and her liver and spleen were nontender. Her skin was normal in color."

The patient tells me, "That young doctor hardly had any time for me. He kept telling me how tired he was and that he needed to see three other patients before he could go home. I started to tell him about my drinking, but I was too embarrassed to admit that I'm an alcoholic. He was in such a rush."

When I examined the patient, I took my time. I noted that her skin was sallow, the whites of her eyes were slightly yellowed, and her liver was enlarged with a tender edge. She was clearly suffering from the ravages of alcohol abuse. Why did I get two stories? The intern wasn't intentionally trying to be untruthful. He just hurried. His story reflected a superficial and inexperienced approach, a very common phenomenon when a patient must be questioned repetitively before the embarrassing truth is revealed. I had the advantage of being more experienced and, therefore, of having been burned many times before.

On another day, a hospital administrator informed me that his E.R. was in disarray because the physician Director was "pissing everybody off." The administrator wanted me to fire him, just like that, without any investigation. He admonished me, "Take my word for it."

The entire episode turned out to be based on a single episode in which a patient, who happened to be the niece of the administrator, had sat in the waiting room for three hours suffering from a migraine headache. It had been a very busy afternoon in the E.R., described by the head nurse as akin to "being under siege."

Invoking "the truth lies somewhere in the middle," I dug further and learned that the physician Director was generally rigid and not communicative. There wasn't a good system to move patients when the E.R. was busy, and the nursing staff was campaigning against the Director because he wanted them all to wear the same color uniforms. But as best as I could tell, the guy was a hard worker, got along well with most of the hospital staff, and was making multiple efforts to improve quality of service. I initiated a series of meetings between the Director, nurses and administrator, and pledged to make changes if they couldn't work out the situation. In doing so, I enlisted the assistance of the administrator, who had felt out of the loop, created a regular path for interaction, and didn't succumb to a knee-jerk snap judgment.

He said, she said. It's all about perceptions and the

spin woven by the storyteller. When you become the recipient of differing views, consciously or subconsciously, the objective of the storyteller is to get you to take a side and make a decision in somebody's best interest. The only way to get an unbiased report is to create a climate of anonymity to gather information. As a manager, you hold the ability to bestow praise, escalate compensation, and advance careers. Likewise, you might become a disciplinarian and take someone down. Therefore, discounting all other extrinsic factors, such as the personal integrity of the historians, *how often you receive an unadulterated report depends more on your track record of being fair in your response than on anything else.* If you want the truth to start in the middle rather than migrate in from the extremes, you must develop a reputation as a person who expects the truth, who listens to all sides, who doesn't automatically jump to conclusions and who responds with dignity. Furthermore, you should reward others who do the same. When you finally understand what truly happened, then consider the impact of any decision you might make. The intern needed to learn to slow down and spend enough time with his patients to be able to evoke the nuances of a complex history and careful physical examination; the E.R. Director needed to become a better communicator and learn how to coordinate services during a "crunch."

You can't be wishy-washy as a doctor, or you will lose patients' confidence. There's a big difference in how people ask for help, depending on whether they feel good or

Paul S. Auerbach, M.D.

they're sick. The more pressured the communication and the more you succumb to the urgency, the greater the risk for biased input. But a doctor is expected to come up with answers. So, understand how you must triangulate on a difficult problem, hone in rapidly, and get on with it. Companies that perseverate and agonize incessantly over strategic direction are like doctors that can't make up their minds—they don't bond with their customers and lose markets to competitors that can find a truth and act on it.

The Patient Who Isn't Screaming
May Be the One in the Most Trouble

A patient who suffers dramatically is easier to diagnose than one who attempts to be stoic. When a person screams in pain and points to her leg, you can be fairly certain where the problem lies, but the gentle optimist who offers only an occasional grimace while her body dips into the danger zone is hiding something horrible and deserves twice the attention.

I vividly remember two victims from the same automobile accident. The first was a burly truck driver, who was swearing profanities. He had a dislocated finger, but was otherwise uninjured. The second was the young woman driver who had been struck broadside by the big man's cement mixer. The door of her vehicle was crushed and she was pinned inside for an hour. When she arrived in the E.R., she'd already been infused with four liters of intravenous fluid. Her only external signs of injury were a cut on her forehead, a bruise on her left flank, and a deformed ankle. When I pressed on her abdomen, she winced and a tear ran down her cheek. Amazingly, she flashed a weak smile and tried to hide her discomfort. Suddenly, her eyes rolled back in her head while her blood pressure plummeted. As she approached unconsciousness, she *apologized* for feeling so bad. Here she was silently bleeding buckets into her pelvis, and *still* trying to be pleasant. Meanwhile, the truck driver was yelling his head off because he wasn't getting any narcotics for his hurt pinky.

It's true that a squeaky wheel gets the grease, but once you've applied some lubricant, the complaining ought to stop. If it doesn't, then you haven't addressed the need or you're dealing with someone who won't be easily pleased. It isn't always readily apparent when suffering is extreme, because sometimes the noise level diminishes as part of the natural progression of the situation. Asthma is a good example. A person in the midst of a mild asthma attack may be wheezing loudly, while the asthmatic on the verge of complete respiratory failure makes almost no noise, because not enough air is moving in and out of the lungs to trumpet a sound. The astute clinician knows how asthma can worsen, and that silence following loud noises can either be very good or very bad.

Someone can vociferously protest a corporate policy and, as a manager, you must respond. Do you agree and side with the employee, or do you maintain the status quo? Let's say you leave things the way they are or apply a small patch. Your employee quiets down. What does that mean? Is the situation better? Is the employee satisfied? Or has the situation grown worse, but nobody is talking any more? Why aren't they talking? Is it because you discourage dissent, that they know that once you've made up your mind the discussion is over, or because the situation has grown so bad that they are, metaphorically speaking, not moving enough air to breathe? What is a doctor supposed to do when someone is very sick and an intervention is made? Reexamine the patient!

Here are the danger signs when stoic behavior indicates weakness, not strength:

1. The inherent problem, if worsened, causes the sufferer to lose strength or motivation.

2. The cure can be toxic.

3. One manifestation of the problem is decreasing ability or desire to communicate.

4. The employee and manager do not "speak the same language."

5. Strength and silence are perceived on a cultural basis to be virtues.

6. Fear has rendered the employee silent.

7. Silence is a manifestation of defiance.

If the buzz from the crowd is loud enough to suppress the one true herald of truth, then put your fingers to your lips and demand silence. But after that, allow everyone to come forward, in public or private, and speak their piece.

Primum Non Nocere

Most managers need to react to a "call to arms." Action, not inaction, is the path to success. But having just said "So, *do something,*" let's consider the flip side. Primum non nocere. It's one of the first things they teach you in medical school. "First, do no harm." The temptation is huge to intervene, to stick in a needle, to throw in a drug. After all, you've got to do something. *You're a doctor.*

If a person isn't dying, you can reflect. Most of the time, you don't have to *do* anything. It may be better to take a deep breath, listen carefully, and let the patient tell you her diagnosis. Physicians are pressured for time, particularly in the E.R., because everybody wants quick results. Action begets reaction. The patient wants to know what's wrong right away, and the nurses want to keep all the patients moving because the waiting room's getting full. You feel compelled to order tests, more than you need really, hoping to find something with a "shotgun" approach. Urgency and haste replace observation and insight. You become committed to a path, and once on that path, deviation slows you down. When you give someone a drug, you invoke the risk of a drug reaction, either irritating and minor or serious and allergic, or perhaps (rarely), even fatal. Could you have waited a bit or withheld the medication? The odds are not in your favor when you're in a hurry.

I'm not afraid to apply the big fix in a critical situation, but I usually try to do as little as possible without becoming a therapeutic nihilist. Over the years I've seen how just about anything can go wrong. Scalpels and medicines are powerful agents for good, but misapplied, are destructive forces as invasive as the worst diseases. Primum non nocere.

How can a manager demonstrate patience on the job? The most common setting for an overreaction is when someone comes to you with a problem or complaint. Something about the situation may provoke you, not to thought and analysis, but to react. You may be of a nature to always seek a quick solution, or you may have scant tolerance for a lackluster performance. Personally, I tend to show less restraint when the problem is repetitive, or if I'm afraid that a passive response will have repercussions. Sometimes I don't have confidence in my ability to manage a worsening situation, so I want to nip it in the bud. There's something to be said for treating bronchitis with an antibiotic before it turns into pneumonia. But that has to be balanced against the fact that most cases of bronchitis are caused by viruses and go away on their own. Whom do you treat and whom do you allow to tough it out? That's a judgment call.

Another way to critique yourself as a manager is to reflect on situations in which you've been criticized for your performance, not for failure to act, but for something you did. Could you have done less or nothing, and been better off? Here are the last three things I did that I shouldn't have done:

1. I criticized my assistant for interrupting me in the middle of an important meeting. She needed me. Instead of listening carefully and being helpful, I responded impatiently.

2. I changed an order placed by my purchasing manager without clearing it through him. I thought I could save a few bucks. He was frustrated by the end run and I wound up with inferior merchandise, because he knew what he was doing in the first place.

3. I voiced a public opinion that a Board member was incapable of changing his immature behavior. I made the mistake of not first asking the opinion of the CEO, who had a personal relationship with this Board member of which I had not been aware. He was boxed in and felt compelled to defend his friend.

In each instance, I was too quick to say or do something. To do no harm, I should have been confident enough to listen and wait.

We all have hot buttons. They provoke us to respond quickly, often in anger or frustration. Those communications may make us feel important, but they're never satisfactory. We need to desensitize ourselves to the words and attitudes that lead us to react emotionally. For me, a real hot button is the suggestion that my ability to multitask means that I'm not paying attention. I get a lot of things done, and I get them done because I can do more than one thing at a time. So, when someone makes me punch a time clock or account for my time, I go nuts. The way I've learned to deal with this is to show what I've accomplished—not how long it took me to accomplish it. Your hot button might be a comment about how you dress or the company you keep, but whatever it is, you can't let yourself be provoked. A patient in the E.R. who angers me by spitting or using abusive language is tempting me to become an incomplete physician. For the sake of that patient, my profession, and myself, I can't allow that to happen. Neither can you.

Don't Count on Luck

When a heroin addict suffers an overdose and stops breathing, he needs an injection of a drug that antagonizes the narcotic and literally restores him to life. In a life-threatening situation, the drug is best administered directly into the victim's vein. The problem is, drug addicts have "used up" their veins by repeated injections of illicit substances laced with dirt and caustic chemicals. Abusive infection and inflammation have caused the most accessible blood vessels to become scarred, shriveled, and impenetrable, even by a sharp needle.

Faced with an unconscious and nonbreathing drug addict on the verge of death, the overwhelming temptation is to grab an intravenous catheter and jam it "blindly" through the skin, hoping to "hit something." Nine hundred and ninety-nine times out of a thousand, that doesn't work. *You can't count on luck in a desperate situation.*

The alternative to luck is preparation, comprised of knowledge, alternatives, and practice. Knowledge begins with a thorough understanding *acquired ahead of time* of the most likely situations you will encounter. When I teach about providing medical care in the wilderness, I always say that the time to learn how to apply splints and bandages is not when you actually need to perform a rescue, but far in advance, in a calm setting where a mistake won't hurt anyone. In business, there are critical situations that sooner or later face every executive—key employee defection, product recall, consumer catastrophe, the ascension of a competitor, and failure to "make the numbers"—and for which there should be a provisional action plan in place. It is infinitely easier to deal with most adverse events, and to teach others during that process, if you are well prepared. Counting on your ability to extemporaneously respond in a very difficult situation can be tantamount to relying upon luck. You don't want to have to do it.

Alternatives are essential. An emergency physician who only knows one way to position a tube or establish an airway is hopelessly restricted. *Improvisation is midway between skill and fortune.* To be creative with regularity is a blessing, but it presupposes that you have the proper intellectual, emotional, and physical resources to pull a rabbit out of a hat over and over again. The successful salesperson learns early to scout a customer and tailor the sales approach. The corporate specialist doesn't rely solely upon salaries and never-ending cash flow, but develops an array of motivational packages that include bonuses, stock options, and promotions.

Finally, practice, practice, practice. True skill applied to a critical situation may appear to be good luck. However, in no profession other than medicine is the phrase, "You make your luck," more true. Often boring routines are the exercises that engrain the absolutely necessary skills into the armamentarium of every competent practitioner. Seize every opportunity to do it, not watch it. Alexandre Karelin, a six-time world Greco-Roman wrestling champion and Olympic legend, advises young wrestlers to "train like a madman," which he says he does "every day of my life." If you are advertised as a leader, remember that when the proverbial excrement hits the fan, everyone will turn to you for the solution, which often means rolling up your sleeves and wading on in. If you don't have the time or aptitude to be good at everything, you should have a plan on how to get help in a relevant time frame. Luck is for the lottery. How many times have you chosen the winning numbers?

So, how do you get the needle into the vein of a drug addict? You learn over time where the "hidden" veins are located, the ones that only a well-prepared healer knows how to find. To hone your skills, you electively slip an I.V. into one of these veins when the situation isn't desperate. Medicine relies upon rehearsal. When the addict stops breathing and the catheter has to go in, you know how to find the vein and can get into it in a minute—or you know how to immediately get someone standing next to you who can do it.

To enhance your luck, seize each opportunity to learn as much as you can about everything that is new, because your best opportunities will come from combining your experiences with what is revolutionary. Create collisions between ideas and good people. The most fundamental business opportunities have arisen in conjunction with the major advances in communication, including the printing press, telegraph, telephone, radio, television, and Internet. Given the right setting, and your ability to be more communicative than your competitors in a noisy environment, the practice will serve you well.

Surround Yourself with the Smartest People You Can, and Work to Make Them Look Good

In my estimation, there are two main types of managers—those who hog the credit when things go well and blame everybody else when things go poorly, and those who distribute credit for success to others, yet accept responsibility for most problems. The first type of manager has trouble retaining the best and the brightest people, because he always takes and rarely gives. The second type is more rare and usually beloved.

The boot camp mentality of medical training, typified by internship, has always seemed to me to be counterproductive. Medical students are chosen for high intellectual capacity, undergraduate achievement, and hopefully, for

Paul S. Auerbach, M.D.

a propensity to be the types of people who will care for patients in situations of extreme intensity and moral complexity. Yet no sooner is an elite group of individuals assembled than it is subjected to a cadre of professors and senior residents-in-training who exploit opportunities to teach by utilizing intimidation. The system imposes unreasonable working hours and ignores the basic human needs of those who are being introduced for the first time to pain, suffering, and death. During internship and residency, sleep deprivation, separation from family and friends, and lack of recreational time become the rite of passage that somehow is supposed to contribute to the making of a fine physician.

So what happens? The tough neophytes handle the pressure and make it through, but more than a few become desensitized to themselves and to their patients. Others are discouraged and abandon medicine as a career because they haven't been eased into a profession in which they might have flourished, had the climate been one of nurture rather than harassment. Looking back at my own training, I recall that I expected to put in long hours and work hard. That was a fair part of the deal. But in return for all of that responsibility, I expected to be taught and made a part of a team. I learned from the drill sergeants, but I learned a lot more from the doctors and nurses who used their skills to make me look good, rather than publicly expose my weaknesses.

It wasn't any different in business school. The best professors drew out their students and found ways to help them express their talents. They focused on displaying the potential inherent in a group of individuals that had been chosen for its leadership qualities, rather than hogging center stage in order to promote their professorial self-worth. The smartest people they could assemble surrounded them, and it was their duty to make *them* look good. In my mind, the harsh taskmasters were insecure and looked at fear as a surrogate for respect. Marines may burnish their muscles in boot camp, but doctors and junior executives mostly achieve exhaustion. The corporate suite is not a battleground, but you'd never know that by the behavior of certain executives and directors. Persons who encounter critical situations need to be able to perform under pressure and function within themselves under conditions of fear, but that doesn't mean that they need to fear their leaders.

One creates a great physician by nurturing and challenging an intelligent person with energy, enthusiasm, compassion, and commitment through an educational process that reinforces the finest elements of the behaviors required to address the perpetual challenge of disease management: scientific rigor, observation, attention to detail, technical proficiency, morality, and concern for the needs of the individual and society. What is different about business, with the exception of a focus upon economics, finance, and marketing? Are loyalty and judicious entrepreneurship (scientific inquisitiveness) bred more strongly in an atmosphere of coaching and support, or in one of recrimination and self-serving autocracy?

There will be an occasional dog performer, disruptive employee, or lazy good-for-nothing individual with whom you must reckon. If you can't make someone adequate, then examine the reasons. If you've inherited mishandled impresarial talent, you still shouldn't be afraid to set clear expectations and performance goals. A wonderful situation is one in which a manager can discover more appropriate placement for an employee within the company that allows mutual prosperity. The satisfied dermatologist who started off as a neurosurgeon is a happy ending to a story that might have ended with a physician-at-heart selling real estate.

Be careful with the All-Stars. Lots of people are great self-promoters and have gotten to the top with smoke and mirrors or frankly manipulative behavior. Whenever you can, build a probationary period of at least six months into your employment agreements. If someone is Attila the Hun, it will usually turn up during that period. And *always* check up on references. You'll be amazed how easy it is to pick up on even the most politely restrained cues from former business associates.

The finest CEOs are surrounded by Vice Presidents that are worthy of the top job, and who are perpetually empowered to build a dominant business machine. Charisma and hubris at the top need to be supported with domain knowledge and impenetrable support networks. In the E.R., while the Chief is negotiating for resources, there are others who maintain the clinical, training, and research operations. These are the future leaders. I have always tried to choose the best, and then give them everything I could for them to be able to excel in their positions. Remember, when it goes well, the credit is all theirs.

A Business Plan Should Be More Like a Care Plan

A care plan is a dynamic method used by an integrated team of medical professionals to provide the best care possible to someone with a specific illness or injury. It might be applied to a person in the hospital for placement of an artificial hip, or to a person with chronic congestive heart failure. The care plan (and the patient it serves) benefits from constant input, including subjective observations from the patient, physiological measurements, test results, and so forth. It's designed to attain the best possible outcome, taking into account all relevant considerations such as the patient's needs, family capability, and financial constraints. To be most effective, a care plan is *continuously* revised to reflect what's possible and desired.

Most business plans are static projections or hypotheses of what might be if the stars line up correctly. They are created to procure funding, and less often written to guide a company through its daily activities. Elaborate spread sheets and assumptions are interspersed with market projections and "guestimates" of how Wall Street

31

will respond to some fabulous new concept or reconfiguration of a less-fabulous old concept. A business plan typically gets a lot of attention for a brief period of time, and then gathers dust on the shelf until its relevance is called into question.

Companies would do better if they had more care plans and fewer business plans. I'm not trying to buck the entire financing establishment. I know that people spending their precious capital need to have something to sink their teeth into. But after the dice have been rolled, take the business plan and turn it into a care plan. Otherwise, your original business plan just becomes an anachronism, or even worse, a blueprint for failure. Take what may have been a solitary process, a vision statement from the entrepreneur, and turn it into something that can be used by a team to actually understand a business and to run it. A working plan works best when there is superb communication, including constant discussion about how each contributor fits into the network of interactions.

I can neither predict the state of your health five years from now nor predict the financial viability of your company and the whims of the public markets five years hence. After you have your stress echocardiogram, your heart-healthy regimen begins. That plan is action-oriented, and minimally predictive. After your company has received its funding, the operations commence. These are also action-oriented, and must be constantly correlated with where you must be on a currently functional, not future, basis.

If It Keeps Bleeding, Move the Bandage

Most people can't stand the sight of blood. Bleeding is one of the most visually distressing medical emergencies. It causes people to panic, faint, or throw up. All of this occurs despite the fact that first aid for a severe cut is "cookbook" and usually successful. In fact, bleeding can be one of the easiest problems to manage, because the treatment is so straightforward.

Your daughter trips and shoves her arm through a window. She sustains a deep cut on her forearm, which bleeds briskly. You lay a couple of gauze pads on top of the wound and press down for a minute. When you lift your hand, you observe that the gauze pads are soaked through, and red blood is dripping from the edges. You grab your first aid book, and it instructs you to pile more bandages on top of the wound and press harder. Don't lift up the bandage, the author tells you, because you don't want to disrupt the blood clotting process. Be patient. You're a good scout, so you follow the instructions and press for another five minutes. To your dismay, the new bandages have soaked through. Beginning to panic, you collect every gauze pad in the house, build a stack a foot high, and squeeze for all you're worth. It still doesn't work. What's gone wrong?

Let's learn some real medicine. How do you stop the bleeding? Have the victim lie down and elevate the bleeding part above the level of the heart. Wear sterile latex rubber gloves or, if you're allergic to latex, nonlatex

33

synthetic nonpermeable gloves. Remove all clothing covering the wound so that you can precisely identify the bleeding source. Almost all external bleeding stops with firm direct pressure. This should be applied directly to the wound with the heel of your hand, using the cleanest available thick bandage or cloth compress. Pressure should be maintained for a minimum of 10 minutes. Normally, peeking at the wound under the compress interrupts the clotting process and prolongs active bleeding. However, *if direct pressure to the wound doesn't stop the bleeding, you must be certain that the pressure is being applied in the correct spot. Simply piling on more bandages will not solve the problem if you're pressing on the wrong spot.*

In the business world, bleeding can take a lot of forms. There's no such thing as therapeutic bloodletting. When the boss comes to you and says, "We've got to stop the bleeding," it usually means that money is being lost, employees or customers are defecting, or there's a string of bad publicity.

Blood is the most precious body fluid. It carries oxygen and energy-laden substances to the tissues, so that an organism may live. What's the equivalent of blood in your business? What carries the energy in your company? It should be the vital enthusiastic efforts of everyone—the communication of spirit and the desire to improve, to find solutions, to be successful. Your company begins to bleed when people become discouraged, disheartened, and jealous. If that happens, *find the wound and repair it!*

No one likes to look at the sticky red liquid, particularly when it's his or her own. This is a particularly important point. World-famous heart surgeons pass out when they cut their finger and watch a drop or two splash on the floor. Your body is programmed to try to get horizontal when you bleed, and for some, the impulse of self-preservation supercedes all conscious efforts to make a more effective intervention. That places an additional obligation on the executive manager to have a plan for self-rescue in place *before* the razor slips and he looks in the mirror.

Every problem in business ultimately has a solution, even if it's to abandon a strategy. Missing financial projections and attracting the ire of analysts is probably as much like a badly bleeding wound as any other type of crisis. You may see a likely fix—raise prices, reduce the payroll, sell a business unit, or some other solution. You follow your plan, keep your fingers crossed, and wait for the next set of numbers. When you're off your projections again the next quarter, it's very tempting to keep your strategy stagnant and, in effect, uncritically pile on the bandages. But don't do it, at least not automatically.

Customers may be leaving you to seek services with a major competitor. So, you make some phone calls, perform a market survey, calculate a few financial ratios, and decide to lower your prices, because your competitor charges less and it seems like this is what's causing the change in allegiance. A sales cycle elapses, and you find that you're losing more market share, now to more than one competitor. They both have lower prices, so you assume that this continues to be the problem. You drop prices further, and in doing so are informed by your regional managers that your margin has now dropped so much that you need to curtail certain services. Fine, you say, the entrails of my M.B.A. pigeon inform me that price is everything in this marketplace, so go with another price cut. You keep losing business, and most of your accounts are in trouble. Where's the error?

You forgot to read the section in the syllabus that said in a situation like this, you should obtain an urgent comprehensive analysis of services. If you were to do this, you would find that your company doesn't allow orders over the Internet, and that your competitors have both deployed Extranets. Your pricing is important, but not the critical issue, because the number one concern for your clients is rapid order fulfillment, best served by the newest communication modalities.

The very first time the blood soaks through the dressing, you need to make a bold move and ascertain if you're holding everything directly over the correct spot. From a strategic business point of view, consider whether you've made the right intervention in precisely the correct location. Have you made the correct diagnosis (it's bleeding, not an allergic reaction, right?), assigned the correct people to the task, given them the resources they need, watched them derive a logical solution, and made a reasonable estimate of the time to cure? It may be that the solution is logical, but you need more pressure (so squeeze harder), but it's equally likely that by moving the stack of gauze to the right just a quarter of an inch (improve your relationship with one key customer), you can turn the situation around. No matter what, continually reassess the situation. Don't be afraid to bring in a skilled specialist if necessary. Pressure will stop most bleeding, but a vascular surgeon who can tie off a major blood vessel is a great person to know when a big artery becomes disrupted.

It makes sense to go with a tried and true solution when a new problem arises, but if it doesn't work like it's supposed to, you have to step back and be analytical, not just keep piling it on. Beating a dead horse is the extreme, but more companies are ruined by tired horses than by expired mammals. Over and over, you'll confirm that change is difficult, and that practice patterns learned during the primary educational process (residency for doctors or business school for managers) are tough to break. This is why it's so useful to add new persons with fresh ideas to your business whenever you can, and then take the time to try to learn from them. The true value of a senior manager or the head doctor in the E.R. is to be able to quickly tell who is sick and who isn't, and then to apply the appropriate resources. Mired in the details, a single manager becomes a micromanager, and the operation runs the risk of bogging down.

Paul S. Auerbach, M.D.

If the Defibrillator Isn't Charged, It Won't Work

A defibrillator device delivers an intense electrical charge to jump-start a quivering, ineffective heart muscle. Sending a power surge through a dying patient's heart is one of the most dramatic moments in medicine, the trailer scene for every media depiction of emergency medicine. But nothing happens if the battery isn't charged. Furthermore, the maneuver only works if it can be deployed successfully within the first four minutes of a cardiac arrest. What good is it if you've never used a defibrillator before, someone's heart stops beating, and you spend ten minutes fumbling around?

For use in an emergency, equipment has to be clearly marked and stored where it's easily accessible. Routines need to be performed with automatic precision, which mandates superlative training and frequent refreshers to keep skills honed. All emergency medical teams practice repeatedly, so that they can apply their skills under the most adverse circumstances. Nerves of steel in the casual classroom setting will otherwise deteriorate into nerves of Jell-O in a real life situation.

You can predict which areas of your business are likely to be affected by a crisis. Improvised crisis management is far less likely to be successful and can be a catastrophic failure. What would you do if your vitamin company had to enact a major product recall because it turned out that a new research study showed that one of your products caused liver cancer? What would you do if your Chief

Financial Officer walked into your office and informed you that he had siphoned the company's 401(k) into an off-shore account? What would you do if your septuagenarian Chairman of the Board clutched his chest and keeled over in a Compensation Committee meeting? What would you do if your major supplier got blown away by a hurricane?

Think about the likely things that can happen to your business and what you would do. Consider who mans the command post, who does the field triage, and who tends to the wounded. Have a disaster plan, let everyone know where it is, and teach them how to use it. Allow your organization to undergo emergency training, and give strong consideration to running a drill from time to time.

Chaos in certain circumstances promotes opportunity, but habitual disorganization is not creative—it's sloppy. More mistakes are made due to lack of preparedness than to bad real-time decisions. I'm not insinuating that regimentation provokes original thought, but rather, that you can approach a situation with spontaneity and creativity and still make good use of structure. Let's manage a horrible airway. If a person is choking and about to stop breathing, the last thing the victim needs is to have everybody running around and shouting over each other in a panic. I like my tubes and drugs lined up, everybody to keep quiet, and a few key individuals to assist me. If I've organized my team well and the "crash cart" is stocked and everything properly labeled, it's no longer an uncontrolled environment. I can deal with that.

It's no different when you're rolling out a new product. Take publication of a book. I've been through this, and lived to tell about it. You can write the best book in the world, someone can go into a bookstore and order it, *Books In Print* can list it, and the computer can show that a distributor carries the book. *But unless the book is physically in the distributor's warehouse, the order has a good chance of being dropped.* All of your expensive publicity efforts will be for naught if someone goes into a bookstore and can't get your book. To be successful, you needed to have gotten the book into the important warehouses prior to your publicity effort. As an electrical charge is essential for the defibrillator to have any effect, distribution into the warehouses and onto the bookshelves is a prerequisite for a book to achieve rapid success.

Pick the Best Athletes

Predicting which undergraduate students will make the best doctors is not easy. Most medical school Admissions Committees use grades, standardized test scores, and essays as screens. Personal recommendations and interviews contribute to a "gut feel" for a candidate. With relatively little knowledge, then, a committee has to make a decision about allowing a person to pursue a career that may have critical impact upon the lives of tens of thousands of other human beings.

Lots of applicants relate weekends as volunteers in hospitals, submit essays describing future lives dedicated to stamping out disease, and have relatives who are orthopedic surgeons. But what have these future doctors done? *Really* done?

The science of medicine is diverse. A person can graduate from medical school and follow a path leading, at one extreme, to care at the bedside for people with terminal illnesses, and at the other extreme, to solitary existence in a research laboratory, interacting only with gene chips and microbes. Professional differentiation usually doesn't occur until after a medical student has had an opportunity to experience and sample many of the options. Therefore, Admissions Committees realize that each and every student must in the course of his or her education interact with suffering human beings, and so they have a responsibility to select for compassion.

After that, the selection process becomes a lot less structured. Do I look for intellectual brilliance, or for a personality that can carry the emotional burden of a dying child? Do I prefer the progeny of a concert pianist or of a thoracic surgeon? Do I value an experienced laboratory assistant or a talented gymnast? These are tough choices.

The considerations are similar in business. How can a recent college graduate really know much about the world? Young adults are commonly undifferentiated, unless they are prodigies. The risk anyone runs with early specialization is excessive premature focus, which can become tunnel vision. I am not advocating that a person who is peripatetic should be rewarded. Rather, I'm

41

suggesting that it's appropriate for a person early in his or her career to be inquisitive, and to want and need to try different things. Just because someone walks into your office and hasn't blown away some sales record in a previous job doesn't mean that this person doesn't have the makings of a fabulous salesperson. *Don't become obsessed with achievements.* Look for desirable qualities.

I like to choose the best athletes. I can teach a very coordinated youngster how to hit a curve ball. I *can't* teach coordination—that's a gift. The major issue in the selection process is just how differentiated a person should be for the task at hand. For the medical student, it's not important if he initially knows whether he wants to be a pediatrician or a pathologist, because there's time to learn, test, and decide. When I'm hiring a faculty emergency physician, however, I need to understand his experience, witness his skills and be comfortable that he can teach. It's no different with a regional sales position. If I'm hiring a trainee, I look for hustle, willingness to learn, and gratitude for the opportunity. On the other hand, the sales manager gets chosen based upon documented productivity, and less on raw potential.

What makes a good athlete? The generic traits are the same in sports, medicine, and business. In order to put together a cohesive team from which may emerge a few superstars, look for the following traits:

- Willingness to listen and learn
- Concern about the task, not compensation

- Ability to complete an assignment
- "Roll-up-your-sleeves" and get-the-work-done attitude
- Noncomplainer
- Understanding of what is ahead
- Multi-tasking ability
- Willingness to share the credit and assume the blame
- At least as much concern for others as for self
- Sense of humor
- Lack of tolerance for failure
- Superb conditioning
- Ability to move past a mistake

How you choose your team depends on where you are in the season. If you need some immediate wins, you should select known performers and expect to pay more. If you're building a team for next season, go with potential and expect to be more of a teacher than a tactical master of seasoned professionals.

We're in the age of electronic commerce, Internet start-ups, and precipitous accumulations (and depletions) of wealth. Young professionals are more often opportunists, and job satisfaction is blatantly subservient to compensation—in particular, to stock options. It used to be that personal income was a strong draw to the medical profession. Today, that is less often the case. When I look at my medical school classmates and see who has changed professions, I observe persons who mostly fall into one of two categories: perpetually curious, or tired and disappointed. When I look at my business school classmates and see who has changed professions, I witness the same: perpetually curious, or precipitously promoted then laid off. The common ground for voluntary change is intellectual curiosity and a desire for professional renewal. Therein lies the blessing and curse of building a great team. In time, the competition desires your best players, and free agency takes over. So, you need to continually strive to understand why people would want to stay with your company, and make it more attractive than the alternatives.

Allow People to Help Solve Their Own Problems

When a patient comes to the E.R., it's likely to be busy, with a long wait to be seen and treated. The doctors and nurses do the best they can to devote attention to each and every person, but it's never enough. What the patients want most is to be cared for, to have attention paid to them, if only intermittently. This care process can be initiated by empowering the patient.

It's best when a patient can be involved in his or her own care. This accomplishes a number of things. First, it requires that a patient receive a thorough explanation of the problem and how an intervention will help improve the situation. Second, it shifts the focus from suffering to resolution. Also, the patient accepts some responsibility for the outcome, rather than adopting a position of total humility. This supports a sense of autonomy and self-worth at a time of vulnerability. It's not a situation of "you got yourself into this, you need to get yourself out of it," but rather an educational process for self-correction. Most of what a doctor does is set the direction. It's up to the patient to follow instructions. Something as simple as holding an ice pack on a painful knee gets the patient engaged and blunts the frustration of delay.

Every manager needs to empower the troops, whether they're lying on a gurney or standing on an assembly line. Helplessness serves no one. The chest surgeon needs to remove the tumor, but the patient needs to take deep breaths, ambulate as vigorously as possible, and wean himself from pain medicines. The Director of Human Resources needs to establish policies and procedures, but it's up to the employees to follow the guidelines and seek ways in which to improve them. When a customer begins to complain about service, who better to analyze the situation, suggest a remedy, and measure the results? If an apology is necessary, should it come only from a manager or from the perpetrator of the insufficiency? If you always think and act for your people, don't expect them to develop brains or brawn.

In emergency medicine, new faculty members have a tendency to be assertive and overconfident. This leads to interpersonal confrontations, which often migrate to the Chief for adjudication. I hate sitting in judgment on these conflicts, which almost always revolve around style rather than substance. Most of the time, I refuse to take sides. My method is to put both people in a room together, listen to both sides of the story (to keep everyone honest), then explain that I expect the combatants to work it out, engaging me as an arbitrator only if they can't resolve the situation themselves. This almost always is successful, because it gets the story straight, usually highlights the trivial nature of the dispute, embarrasses everybody involved, and puts forth the notion that highly trained professionals should be responsible for their actions.

It's a Whole Lot Worse to Lose a Patient Than to Not Get a Patient

When I say losing a patient, I don't mean having someone die. What I mean is losing a patient to a competitor, having a patient leave your practice because of dissatisfaction with your service, or worst of all, suing you for malpractice. Each of these implies failure, a relationship squandered, negating whatever hard work went into establishing the bond in the first place. Furthermore, one dissatisfied customer tells at least ten other persons of their frustration, while the happy patients generally keep satisfaction to themselves.

In this day and age of declining loyalties and innumerable choices for goods and services, it takes a Promethean effort to build a customer base. Thus, it's particularly painful when a loyal customer leaves because you can't compete on service. The amount of energy that goes into marketing can be considerable, and in businesses such as medicine, in which longitudinal relationships are essential, losing customers negates an effort that spanned considerable time and expense. Furthermore, once a person has a bad experience and switches, it is not likely that they will switch back, because bad experiences tend to linger.

How does one keep from losing a valued client? *I believe the best way to accomplish this is to make a continual effort to get inside your client's head* and understand the current state of needs. A patient's needs for health-care services change over time. This concept is not appreciably different in other business settings, unless you are dealing with a solitary supply and demand situation.

In the Internet land grab where first-to-market (successfully) has in certain circumstances equated with winner-take-all, you simply cannot expect lost customers to give you a second chance. Some of the huge franchise companies may get away with a recall from time to time, but not without the expense of allowing a struggling competitor to get back in the game. However, you must have a sustainable business model (a good attitude will suffice for openers) that stems from understanding what your customers need for which they are willing to pay.

The final insult that occurs when you lose a customer is a breach of proprietary advantage. It's very common for the customer to share all that is known about how you do business with your replacement, for the purpose

Paul S. Auerbach, M.D.

of avoiding a repeat of whatever was unsatisfactory. The
net effect is to reveal not only your flaws, but also your
business methods. So, *don't lose customers!*

Don't Tolerate Bad Behavior,
Even from Your Patients

The customer is king. The customer is always right.
Always stay focused on your customer. The mantras of a
service business have only in recent years begun to
imprint on health-care professionals. In a department
store, the clerks are trained to anticipate the needs of
their customers, and to react to their wants, whims, and
moods. This includes dealing with disappointment, frustration, and anger. After all, what the customer feels and
says must be correct.

This is much more of a challenge in an environment
in which the customers are miserable and frightened.
Doctors and nurses are trained to forgive hostility and
negative emotional outbursts, attributing them to the
voices of pain and suffering. This is a feature of the profession that everyone accepts as part of doing business.
We all achieve a certain level of tolerance for bad
behavior, and ascribe as much of it as possible to the
situation, rather than take it personally, lose our temper, and react in a way that might jeopardize the doctor-patient relationship.

Shame on me, but some customers just aren't worth it.
Everyone who comes to the E.R. is legally entitled to a

thorough evaluation if there's a chance that medical attention is necessary. However, just because you're a patient in the E.R., you're not entitled to abuse the staff or other patients. Loud, drunk, and obnoxious individuals deserve to be shown the exit the same way they would in any other public venue. Someone who is grief-stricken is entitled to wide latitude in behavior, but someone who is impatient and unruly is not entitled to curse a nurse or throw a punch at a doctor. When a nasty patient proclaims, "You have to take care of me," the answer may be, "No, I don't." It's even appropriate to have a truly abusive patient arrested for disorderly conduct. By establishing a controlled and safe work environment, I am benefiting the greatest number of persons, including staff and patients.

The same is the case with abusive customers or clients. As much as I would like to maintain certain accounts, there are situations that I cannot abide. These include blackmail, dishonesty, foul language, intimidation of my employees, and foolish threats of legal action. All of these reflect a lapse in a good faith relationship and definite lack of business acumen, which are harbingers of worse to come. I can assure you from experience that a person who lies once will lie again, a bad check bounced is indicative of a rubber account, and the customer who loses his temper over an insignificant event will become an absolute idiot when a true crisis arises. Build your business around reasonable people, and show respect for your employees by running interference for them with the jerks. Nothing shows strength better than defending your people when they come under attack from disruptive individuals.

Before I bark back, I always try to give my patient or customer the benefit of the doubt and try to see if there's justification for their behavior. That can be tough when a drunken loudmouth in the E.R. is harassing me. On the other hand, I've learned that a sober obnoxious complainer can be a very astute observer. Similarly, the grumpy malcontent employee is perhaps more tuned into your company's flaws than the uncritically happy employee, so control the abuse, but listen carefully.

The extreme form of unacceptable patient behavior is a hostage threat. Never get held hostage. The first time I refused to care for a patient, I was working in the E.R. on a busy Saturday night, juggling the care of a lot of people. One of my patients was a little old lady with a superficial cut over her eyebrow. The bleeding had stopped. She was obviously well to do, sporting large diamond rings and a treasure trove of gold bracelets. When I got to her, she was annoyed at having had to wait her turn and commented that "those other people ought to be made to wait." She was pretty cranky.

I wanted to close her wound with stitches. I numbed the skin with a local anesthetic and covered her face with sterile drapes, so that only her eyebrow was exposed. I left a tunnel of cloth over her mouth so that she could breathe and talk. As I prepared to advance the needle for her first stitch, she said, "You'd better do a good job."

I replied, "I'll do the best job I can. We always try to do the best job we can."

Her response was swift and had an edge to it. "You'd better do a good job or I'll sue you."

Her words were inappropriate and insulting. They weren't meant to be humorous. She was trying to intimidate me, perhaps to express her frustration at having had to wait. Maybe she was just a mean old lady. I didn't care.

I lifted the drapes from her face and asked her to open her eyes. "I'm going to have the nurse come in now and bandage your face. Then you are free to leave. There won't be any charge. I'm afraid that I can't be your doctor."

The woman angrily informed me that I was obligated to care for her. I responded that I was obligated to care for her if she had a true emergency, but that her words were foolish, her threat unnecessary, and that she had violated our relationship with her careless and unnecessary comment. Furthermore, there was another hospital close by from which she was free to seek care. She asked to speak the doctor in charge. When I told her that was me, she stormed out and marched up to hospital administration, where, lucky for me, they told her the same thing.

Everybody likes a satisfied customer, but there are limits. I always advise everyone to bend over backwards to make a customer or patient happy, but that isn't always possible. No leader who wishes to set an example ever allows himself to be taken hostage, unless it serves a very strategic purpose.

Paul S. Auerbach, M.D.

You Need to Be Able to Differentiate between a Pimple and Cancer

This speaks to technical capability, something that any doctor loses over time unless he practices often enough. When my friends ask how to choose a physician, I tell them to find someone at least five to ten years posttraining—young enough to still be enthusiastic about medicine and close to the latest advances, yet experienced enough to bring maturity to the practice. Unless a physician stays busy and regularly pursues continuing education opportunities, he will become set in his ways. Deterioration of medical knowledge occurs more rapidly in persons unfamiliar with new technology and who are computer illiterate. Deterioration of manual skills occurs more rapidly in persons who teach (they watch, instead of "do") and who do not pursue enough clinical time to support dexterity and acumen.

As a person ascends the management ladder in medicine, administrative responsibilities force substitution of meetings for surgeries, financial reports for medical journals, and offsite "retreats" for medical seminars. Clinical sharpness wanes in exchange for value as an administrator. Therefore, one of the first responsibilities of an astute medical manager is to be certain that the practitioners are solid and the medicine remains excellent. In order to do that, the presumption is that a person who once was technically competent can recognize when everyone is doing a good job. The farther you wander from clinical practice, the more you are forced to rely upon assessment by others. That's a disadvantage. Therefore, it's mandatory to either maintain basic competence in your field, or to have a trusted someone who can do that for you.

All the above holds true in business. *It's easy to ascend the corporate ladder and forget the details of operations that served as your proving ground.* It's also a natural tendency to believe that all of the agonies of training and disrespect heaped upon you as a rite of passage must be replicated in order for the next generation to prove itself. That's nuts, unless harsh treatment served a real purpose. One has to keep a finger on the pulse of the business, but take care not to press so hard as to cut off the circulation. If a senior manager wants to be effective, he must be a teacher and learn to focus energy on persons willing to learn. These expectations are reasonable and can be enforced. Anyone who won't respond to a cogent educational effort presented in a collaborative fashion can be justifiably dismissed.

The venture capital community prides itself on being able to offer "added value" to companies in which it invests. This is in the form of opening doors, mentoring the executive team, and donating sage advice based upon having "been there and done that." In many cases, the "VCs" live up to this claim, but it's very difficult to do more than hit the high points when you're sitting on the Boards of fifteen companies, reviewing hundreds of business plans, and trying to meet tight deadlines for investing many millions of dollars. What eventually suffers in an extreme multi-tasking environment is attention to detail. You get so busy that when something goes in your right ear, something falls out your left ear. When you find that you are constantly hypothesizing, estimating, and rounding off, it's time to bring in someone to do the detail work.

Grow old gracefully. As a good physician friend and former outstanding athlete recently told me, "It's tough to go from having a 41-inch chest to having a 41-inch waist." If you're a senior executive, quit trying to flex your muscles when you should be keeping your shirt on. Recognize that your value as a mentor is to understand how your business works, put great employees to work, support them, and focus on the strategies, relationships and customers that require your seasoned fund of knowledge.

It's More Difficult to Make a Diagnosis When Your Patient's in a Coma

When a patient's unconscious, you don't ask where it hurts because there's no opportunity for dialogue. Worse yet, you *know* that since your patient is in a coma, something is terribly wrong, and it's critical for you to make the diagnosis. But nobody's talking. What happened? Where does it hurt? Have you ever been sick like this before? Without a verbal inquiry, you must resort to a handicapped physical examination, lab tests, and radiological studies to figure out what's gone wrong.

Medical diagnosis requires a phenomenal amount of communication. An unconscious person can be suffering from a stroke, heart attack, drug overdose, brain hemorrhage, meningitis, low blood sugar—the list goes on and on. A person with a swollen ankle may have a sprain, be victimized by congestive heart failure, suffer from extreme kidney disease or arthritis, or be in the throes of a serious bacterial infection. Doctors acquire clues to reach a diagnosis, classically by talking, observing, touching, and testing. Without effective verbal communication, the remainder is more difficult and may follow many blind alleys.

It's obvious that a patient in a coma can't complain that it hurts when the doctor presses on his swollen belly, or relate that yesterday he fell off a ladder onto his left side, rupturing his spleen. But it's less obvious how the usual doctor-patient communication inhibits communication, when everyone is able to speak the words. Many doctors are in a hurry. When a typical doctor takes an initial history from a patient, he or she interrupts the patient within the first minute of the interview. It has been shown that after this initial interruption, most patients never get a chance to finish their stories. The remainder of the conversation is led by the physician, who's in a rush to reach an end point, usually scribbling a few notes and ordering a bunch of tests while conversing. What way is that to interact with a person who is suffering, scared, in need of explanations, and completely vulnerable to the decisions of the practitioner? It's discourteous at best and dangerous at worst.

Paul S. Auerbach, M.D.

So who's in a coma, the patient or the doctor? If a patient can't communicate effectively, which includes confiding delicate information often withheld in embarrassment or because the patient doesn't understand what's important, the medical implications can be severe. If the doctor presses ahead on a predetermined path wearing blinders, he will drive past the correct diagnosis and obligate the patient to a more prolonged course of evaluation and treatment. If the doctor doesn't draw out the patient's concerns and dig into the subtle aspects of the illness, then he in essence is forcing the patient to be simplistic and noncommunicative.

Many employees and managers don't communicate either, and might as well be in a coma for all the guidance they give you about your business. This is never productive, and signifies that something is wrong, much like the illness that has rendered a patient silent. A person who is innately shy can be coaxed out into the open and made to recognize the value of full disclosure. However, the person who is tight-lipped by intention is either masking a fundamental suffering or hasn't been made to recognize the value of bringing personal thoughts to bear in a constructive manner.

As a leader in your organization, you must encourage regular open discussions of important issues, if for no other reason than to recognize that something is wrong when everyone quiets down. You can do this with almost any discussion, even politics, if need be. People need to

56

learn to engage in useful dialogues—it is not an innate ability for most persons.

From time to time, your employees are on the verge of a "corporate coma." That is, a business unit can be failing and all the symptoms of breakdown can be present while the cause is unknown. Sometimes a person can walk into your office and make the diagnosis, "I shipped the computers to the wrong address and the customer's furious," but more often, you have an angry client for no apparent reason. Another time, a senior manager will tell you that his unit is failing, morale is low, and performance targets cannot be met. You ask him why and he throws up his hands to answer, "I don't know." In each situation, you need to be able to gather information and draw out the details. This takes communication skills that exceed the ordinary and that can move past guilt, fear, self-recrimination, and deception. If you are inherently heavy-handed, your staff won't open up to you and the organism may fail before you can determine the cause of the problem.

With my patients, I always start with the question, "Are you in pain?" This accomplishes two things—it establishes that I care about the patient and it begins to point me in the direction of the root cause of the problem. Sometimes the pain can be "referred" from one location to another, which is the reason that someone with a sore throat has an earache, even when the ear exam is normal. In your company, the lost account might reflect something as obscure as a rude telephone clerk, but your investigation will get to the problem sooner or later. After you figure out where it hurts, ask the patient how long the pain has lasted and what brings it on. Finally, ask what makes the pain go away. In your business, follow the same line of reasoning (Who's upset? When did you find out about this? Have you done anything to make the situation better? Did it work?). Note that very little of this is intervention. Rather, it is all historical information gathering, data to be factored into the decision you will make about where the problem lies and how best to deal with it.

Also, don't be afraid to wake everybody up. How many meetings have you endured where the front row was nodding off, heads bobbing like marionettes on a string? You can't get anything done until they're paying attention. Open the window and let some cold air in, lead the group in a stretching exercise, or pass the wet towels and let everybody wash their face.

Some People Are Dead When They're Cold and Dead

Hypothermia is a condition of lowered body temperature. Unless a victim is found frozen in a block of ice or has been recently pulled from frigid waters, the most likely clue to a hypothermic state is altered consciousness. In fact, a person who is severely hypothermic may appear to be dead, but still be alive. This is because hypothermia can be protective, in that the victim may not require a "normal" heart rate, breathing rate, or blood pressure. There have been documented cases of "miraculous" recoveries from complete cardiac arrest associated with environmental hypothermia, presumably because of the protective effect of the cold. From these events has arisen the aphorism, "No one is dead until he is warm and dead."

However, some people are dead when they're cold and dead. That is, they were dead before you ever started the resuscitation. How do you tell which is which? Is there any way to distinguish the person who is cold and will live from the one who is frozen and will die? Not very well. The result is a conundrum of life-and-death importance, complicated by the fact that attempting to perform a prolonged resuscitation in a harsh, cold environment can pose significant danger to the rescuers, and consume precious (and expensive) resources.

The rescuer must combine medical knowledge with search and rescue wisdom. He must weigh the needs of the victim against the needs of the many. I don't have a perfect answer, except to say that had I been able to recognize impending hypothermia, perhaps the victim would never have slipped into this predicament.

When a business unit is cooling off, could I have recognized its demise sooner, and made a critical intervention before it froze solid? Only if I was familiar with the signs and symptoms of deterioration, and was paying attention. When one of my managers is caught in a winter storm, begins to undress, and says, "Don't worry about me, I'll be OK. Just leave me behind," should I leave him to fend for himself? Never!

Still, some situations are beyond salvaging, and that's when you have to grit your teeth and cut your losses. When the life forces are gone, then the business is dead. If you are willing to risk the rest of the business in a resuscitation attempt even when you understand that the odds are against you, you might make the decision to try for a save. But if the situation is beyond repair and diverting your best people is most likely to fail, you need to give it up, for everyone's sake. Some businesses are dead when they're cold and dead.

See One, Do One, Teach One

Young doctors and medical students soon learn that the educational process is "See one, do one, teach one." In their enthusiasm for access to patients and their rush to independence, students are eager to become "real doctors," to sew up a cut or deliver a baby, not just to read about it. I remember that the Catch-22 of medical school was that you needed to have done something in order to be allowed to do it. There was no provision for the first-time experience. So, you studied the steps and learned all the details so that you could pretend to be competent, and then hoped that the intern was tired enough to offer you the procedure and wouldn't notice how badly your hands were shaking. After you had done it once, you were deemed sufficiently knowledgeable to teach somebody else.

The flaw in this tradition is obvious, but it goes on today, in the hospital and inside your company. It ought to be "See one, learn one, do a few, then teach one." Teaching can become tiresome, but day in and day out, it's probably the most important service a manager provides. Proper teaching requires some appraisal of effectiveness, whether it's through a test or mere observation. You haven't fulfilled your responsibility as a teacher until you are assured that your student has actually learned the material. Recitation of the principles is not learning—it's memorization. I want to see someone actually do it, preferably under trying circumstances. Anyone can throw a few stitches in a wound and make it look neat when the cut is straight, there's no bleeding, the patient is sedated, and there's a nurse to hand over instruments. It's another story when a chunk of flesh has been taken out by a dog bite, blood is pouring everywhere, the patient is drunk and swinging at you, and you're on your own. Handling a situation under adverse conditions, where improvisation is essential, represents a real achievement. To determine what your people have learned, watch them in action. Place them in tough situations and see what they can do. If you are willing to teach, there is always someone willing to learn.

Nonproductive Chaos Evolves into Organized Dissention; Productive Chaos Yields New Discoveries

Everyone strives for a creative environment in which ideas flow freely and workers are motivated to develop new ideas and translate creativity into business opportunities. History regales us with stories of serendipity and how chance favors the prepared mind. Some even look to chaos, the absence of structure, in which to brew innovations and scientific advances.

The student of science knows that for every discovery that falls out of the sky, there are hundreds that form from organized efforts. Planning and strategy are not anathema to creativity, but rather, form the milieu in which true creativity can flourish. Furthermore, as the science of medicine advances, the opportunities for unplanned discovery perhaps diminish. There are undiscovered pharmaceuticals in tropical jungles, for sure, but without a systematic approach to their discovery, they will rarely be identified. It's hard to imagine that the antidote to virulent viruses will come from mold on a loaf of bread, or that new surgical instruments will be designed without the use of sophisticated computer-aided design.

People who operate in service organizations need structure as well, particularly when change is necessary. Without an environment in which tools can be brought to bear upon complex situations, the results are often unpredictable and suboptimal. Without leadership, group behavior tends to be chaotic and nonproductive. So, there is a correct amount of guidance necessary for any group to function. Worse than disorganization is rebellion or subversive activity, which can follow an exchange between strong dissenting egos over a difficult decision. Simply put, somebody needs to be in charge.

This is well known in the frenetic environment of an E.R., where crises abound and tension runs high. The trauma victim is brought in, mangled and bleeding. Medical professionals are trained not to panic, but that's difficult when organs are exposed and the patient is choking to death. Everyone reaches for the tube at the same time, yet each wants to place it in his own way. Should the x-ray be taken first or should the patient be rolled to expose his back? Is one intravenous line sufficient or should there be two? What antibiotic is most appropriate to kill the germs that will invade the torn limb? Opinions fly, voices are raised, and unless there is a strong leader, the din of anxiety creates an atmosphere of confrontation rather than collaboration. In the presence of a "trauma captain," the process runs smoothly and each person has a role. Chaos is not transformed into tranquility, but it becomes manageable.

In a corporation, where there's a completely open environment with little structure, there's a tendency to confuse lack of hierarchy with lack of organization. The essential framework allows a free flow of ideas that can be documented for current or future use. Policies and procedures are useful during times of routine activity and when there is intense activity. They are not designed to promote creativity, but certainly shouldn't inhibit it. Furthermore, faced with a complex task, employees may become frustrated by lack of structure. Probably the single most important functional trait admired in a leader is the ability to take charge and bring useful order to a chaotic situation. This can be the strategy necessary to save a life, win a battle, or drive a company to success.

Know Your ABCs

In emergency medicine, the ABCs are airway, breathing, and circulation. These involve therapies and interventions that have to be knee-jerk responses, not something you need to look up. If a person needs an airway, isn't breathing, has an ineffective heart, or is in shock, it's a true emergency. Any competent emergency physician can insert an endotracheal tube through someone's vocal cords, make an emergency incision through someone's cricothyroid membrane to place a tube directly into the trachea through the neck, perform mouth-to-mouth or bag-valve-mask breathing, complete the chest compressions of CPR, and start I.V.'s fifteen different ways in order to administer intravenous fluids and medications. Furthermore, these can be done quickly, definitively, and without referring to Chapter 2 in a handbook.

What are your ABCs? What do you have to be able to do on instinct? If you're the CEO, you need to be able to orchestrate a financing when the IPO market turns cold. If you're the COO, you need to be able to manage your most important customers when you have to initiate a major recall that's going to impact their businesses. If you're the CFO, you need to be able to understand your financials so that you can preach the numbers effectively on every conference call. If you're the Director of Human

Resources, you need to know the drill when someone files against your company on the basis of harassment or discrimination. If you're the Director of Information Technology, you need to be able to bring the network up in sixty minutes when a virus hits one hour before your biggest yearly promotion.

Individuals Quit One at a Time before the Team Goes on Strike

In health care, the trend has been to move away from individual approaches in order to support a team approach. In the E.R., we have teams that respond to trauma patients, critically ill children, victims of sexual assault, and major behavioral disorders. This is in recognition of the need for a coordinated approach to complex presentations and the necessity for the application of unique skills. Other groups of caregivers are clustered by specialty and become bargaining units—nurses, therapists, and technicians. Unions may emerge, and even include physicians. In the midst of every hospital union is someone who is dissatisfied, and prepared to forego long-term professional relationships and patient care for a victory on labor issues.

A nimble manager ought to be able to smell discontent a mile away, but how often does that happen? We become distracted by our daily successes, and don't spend enough time looking for the warning signs. It's really simple enough, if you know what to look for. The first sign of impending insurrection is when teams that are supposed to be functioning cohesively to produce something begin to bicker internally, and then to complain externally. The second sign is when an individual quits. By quitting, I don't mean leaving for career advancement or to pursue a dream. I mean leaving the job because the pay isn't sufficient, there's low morale, no rest for the weary, or all the assorted other factors that cause a job to be a bummer. In health care, continuing to work with poor performance ends in more than a loss of pride, because no matter how unhappy an employee is with the working environment, the patients' needs remain the same. When a health-care worker's quality declines, someone needs to move quickly to find out the source of the problem before there is an adverse outcome.

Perhaps all you do when someone leaves their job in your company is arrange for an exit interview. I don't have much confidence in these, because in the interview the agenda of the person quitting is often to generate a decent recommendation for the next job. Furthermore, persons who leave because they are intimidated rarely trust the evaluation process. A lack of confidentiality or a despot at the CEO level renders impotent the justice of disclosure. Frankly, most people need their jobs and are willing to put up with some pretty aberrant management practices to keep them. They are afraid of the senior management networks and feel trapped within a corporate malignancy.

If you're not a tyrant and are open to constructive resolutions in your organization, then here's how it should work. The person who resigns should be interviewed without any innuendo of recrimination to find out everything he or she thinks and feels about the company, the job, and the people in the immediate work setting. Someone with human resources experience should process the information, check its veracity, and use it to evaluate its applicability to constructive processes, which include communications to employees and modifications of business practices. When more than one person resigns, particularly when there is known to be conflict, the analysis is more imperative, and should be completed vigorously. If you don't have the professional wherewithal to accomplish this internally, bring in a professional. By the time a problem is sufficiently intense to cause multiple resignations, it is capable of altering the fabric of your company, and ruining *your* career as a senior manager.

If You Gamble, Be Prepared to Lose

"No risk, no reward." "No bravery, no blue chips." "The biggest victories go to those who are willing to put it all on the line." How many times have you listened to these spirited challenges? How many of you have posters on your walls that encourage you to reach the summits of the world's tallest peaks?

There are circumstances in which risk is the only inspiration that can move a person forward. I vividly recall offering a cancer patient the choice between no therapy (certain death with gradual deterioration over a one-year period) and difficult chemotherapy (possible prolongation of life for an additional year *or* failure and rapid death over six weeks). Tough choice, and a definite gamble. The chooser had to be prepared to lose. She opted for the treatment and lived for a year. It could easily have gone the other way.

At the senior management level, your day should be one of decisions. The delegator fashions himself as a decision maker, and operates from informed advice. The strategist also accumulates information, but engages more in the synthesizing process, which leads to direct responsibility for what happens. Both types of individuals can be effective, so long as there is strength in operations. Somehow, the work has to get done.

The gambler is a risk taker compelled by personality traits that you should not seek to replicate in a business model. Gamblers are compulsive by nature, and look for a jackpot type of return or windfall on a lucky decision. What most gamblers forget or repress is the fact that the foundation of success in the gambling industry is based upon the overwhelming majority of losers, who supply rewards for the infinitesimally small number of big winners. Gambling in business should be considered a desperation move, only attempted in a last-ditch effort to succeed when the alternative is guaranteed abject failure. Furthermore, one should only gamble when one is prepared to lose, because failure is the most likely outcome.

In medicine, a pure gamble is totally unacceptable. Calculated risk, in which informed parties understand the odds, the risks and rewards, and the consequences of failure, can be allowed under certain circumstances. When a farmer comes to me with a severed index finger, torn from his hand by a grain thresher, he asks me what should be done. I inspect his wound and observe that the detached finger is broken in three places, the tissue edges have been crushed, straw and fertilizer are ground into the stump, and that it has been seven hours since the injury occurred. It is extremely unlikely that reimplantation of his injured finger will be successful, and much more likely that the attempt will generate a serious infection. Even if the finger "takes," the farmer will be plagued by a rigid finger without sensation, crooked and nearly useless. He'd be better off to accept his loss and adapt to a four-fingered hand.

However, the decision is his. I can advise against reimplantation, but am bound to inform him that there is a very small chance for a miraculous outcome, which would be a functioning, useful finger and no wound complications. The choice is his. I am willing to find a hand surgeon, who will explain again that there is extremely little chance that the repair will turn out the way the farmer hopes.

When you're running a company, you take many calculated risks. Pilot projects that don't telegraph your intentions to the competition are a big help to determine what will and won't work. However, they have to be performed under realistic conditions that mimic what might happen on a larger scale. You may decide that your chain of ice-cream stores will benefit from the introduction of jalapeño pepper sundaes, but unless you have proven it with some preliminary marketing or have some *experience,* it sounds like a gamble to me. And as much as we kid around about doing things with "OPM" (Other People's Money), you really are on dangerous ground when your burn rate exceeds the capacity of your company's fire extinguishers.

It Only Hurts When I Laugh

Sunday morning in the E.R. is often a peaceful time. The craziness of Saturday night has wound down and hangovers take precedence over acute intoxication. Some patients sleep late, while others spend the early hours in church. If there's ever an easy time to work in the E.R., it's Sunday morning.

I was reading the newspaper when the head nurse grabbed me in a panic and pulled me into the trauma room. The paramedics were laboring over a young man who was bleeding profusely from his head. His scalp was sliced wide open in an arc that started between his eyebrows and ended at the vertex of his balding dome. There was a groove in the outer table of his visible skull, and the wound was laden with shards of bone and chips of wood. Thank God I didn't see any brain. As I worked feverishly to apply compression clips to staunch the red torrent, I asked him, "Does it hurt?," to which he replied, "Only when I laugh." He was blinded by the blood, but chuckled and winced. "Hey Doc, I'll bet you can't guess how I did this." He wasn't drunk, just tickled by something.

"No, I can't. What happened?"

"Am I gonna live?" He grinned at the nurses.

"I think so." I fingered the trench in his skull. "How the heck did you do this?"

"Well, I was stickin' a piece of plywood into a table saw." He leaned forward to demonstrate. "And then I stuck my head right into the saw! Guess that was sumpthin', huh?"

He looked to me for approval, and I noticed a "Born To Lose" tattoo on his shoulder. "Guess you fulfilled your prophecy." I shook my head and we both started laughing.

What a dumb move, but what a great attitude. Think how phenomenal it is to face a personal crisis, and to try to see the humor in it. He didn't take his situation lightly, because he called for a rescue, but he knew that what was done was done.

Not everybody in an awful situation dwells on the dark side. We expect people to be serious, frightened, judgmental, heroic, or morose in a crisis. We are surprised by persons who can evoke humor at a time like this. If suffering consistently strikes you as funny, then you are losing your emotional equilibrium, but if you can remain positive or even happy when everyone around you is losing it, then you'll probably be a more effective leader and live a lot longer.

Things go wrong in business all the time, and often there are sudden, foolish errors. I've made them, you've made them—we all make them. Of course, we need to find solutions, and when there's bad blood, the logical expressions are of anguish, not mirth. The sooner you can get to a position where your perspective allows you a smile or a laugh, the sooner your pain is transformed from a situation of crisis and decline to one of optimism and healing. As much as pain is a protective mechanism, laughter is one of recovery. The two work together very nicely. When you grimace in anguish, you are a victim; when you smile in the face of adversity, you're brave (when you're not clueless).

Let your ego run second to your good nature, and you'll be surprised at how often you can be perceptive instead of tough and still remain in control of a situation. A well-timed smile or even a joke can do much to soften a situation, so long as it is not offensive. If the people around you don't want to be happy, that's their problem. This isn't "Don't worry. Be happy." I want you to "Worry, but be happy."

Are You Having Any Fun?

At this point in your reading, take a moment and reflect on your job. Are you having any fun? I really enjoy practicing medicine. It's great to work hard with a team of individuals who dedicate themselves to taking care of people, 24 hours a day, seven days a week. We save lives, deliver babies, relieve pain, and counsel elite CEOs and the homeless alike, all in the course of a single business day. I wouldn't trade the fascinating career I've had in the E.R. for any other profession in the world. On a moment-by-moment basis, there is intensity and high emotion, but in the aggregate, it's very manageable and stimulating.

What about you? Are you doing something worthwhile? Do you come home from work each day feeling that in some way, you've made life better for someone? Have you been cheerful? Have you been a good teacher? Have you helped someone through a difficult situation? Have you had a creative moment or helped someone make an important decision?

Are you having any fun?

THE DOCTOR

A physician is a leader. Trained in science first and in social skills to a lesser degree, doctors are nonetheless expected to be perfect. After your family, your doctors hold your highest trust. What features of a physician should be emulated by a corporate executive? First and foremost, concern for the customer. Beyond this, I expect company leaders who are paid enormous financial rewards to maximize shareholder value (help the patient mend and thrive), show integrity, stay current, support their employees, teach, communicate, and be willing to make personal sacrifices. Observations of my own and other doctors' behavior confirms my contention that the lessons learned taking care of patients can often be applied in a business setting. Like an orchestra needs a conductor, a hospital needs physician leadership. The finest companies make their greatest progress when they are led brilliantly. In this section, the focus is on the individual.

Doctors Are Creatures of Habit

Medical education and training impart habits based as often on opinions as facts. It's believed that lack of adherence to improved and logical diagnostic standards leads to excessive utilization, such as over-ordering of tests and unnecessary interventions. To combat this phenomenon, there is a trend toward "evidence-based medicine." In a contemplative moment, no physician would disagree that he has much to learn (always!) about new drugs, techniques, tests, and the relationships between clinical methods and outcomes. However, it takes twice the effort to influence someone who is both busy and comfortable in his practice to adopt a new way of doing things (change) as it does to convince the novice of the wisdom of that same approach. When we are vacant sponges, we are taught "the way things are." In that process, we become skeptics, because we become opinionated. Later on, as we become less inquisitive and move from learning into practice, it's more difficult to adopt a new style or give credence to a novel approach. We feel we can get by with what we know and may even resent having to maintain the effort necessary to keep up with the new knowledge pouring out of the labs and research wards.

Because of the frenetic pace of an E.R., everyone who practices there on a regular basis develops his or her own work flow process. Some doctors like to see the patients as soon as each is put in a room, and make a rapid assessment of who's sick and who isn't. Others like to stay focused on a single person and minimize "multi-tasking," relying upon the nurses to sound the alarm if someone is in need of more attention. Yet others prefer to have the patients screened by the medical students, allowing them to work independently and to act as a filter for the faculty. Layered upon these styles is how one creates the medical record. Some physicians like to write, some like to dictate, a few use computers, and some like to have a scribe follow them around to record like a stenographer. Each method can be further broken down by refinements of the process—do I prefer to write during the exam, immediately after the exam, or at the end of the day, when I am completely finished seeing patients? You get the idea. I have a work flow process best suited to me, which I've modified only for episodic constraints imposed by the E.R. environment. I am a creature of habit. Anything labeled as an "advance" or "improvement" is first met with skepticism, because I find it difficult to change.

It's absolutely no different in business unless there's a corporate commitment to education and change, both of which require time and resources. Learning doesn't just happen—it has to be supported by the behaviors of senior managers and the policies they support to make it happen. The critical tension is between performance and productivity on the one side, and time and measures of performance on the other side. When people try out new techniques, the learning curve precedes improvements. The only way to avoid this is to run parallel operations, the old against the new, until everyone is up to speed. That requires duplicate resources.

Is it reasonable to expect your employees to allocate nonwork time to job-related self-improvement? Probably, if the effort has implications for broader life issues, such as competence and self-esteem. However, a voluntary education policy means that a certain, perhaps large, number of workers will not take the time to study the issues that are of greatest importance to your business. Even if they do, they'll approach the educational process in a perfunctory manner. It's better, I think, to allow the efforts to occur in the workplace or in another setting at the company's expense. This sends a strong message, and guarantees that the education is appropriate and well presented. A fatal flaw in many companies occurs by neglecting development of existing employees, opting for the new hire to replace a person with outdated skills. This is a sorry commentary on our ability to appreciate employees and reflects an expedient alternative to the more complex, but ultimately more stabilizing, educational process. Every manager should have a plan of education and training with a career path for each employee, unless a position is deemed to be purely unskilled labor.

Even in this setting, a company grows stronger by promoting from within, if it can encourage its workers to be just as eager as a person new to the organization. Creativity in business requires that muscles be exercised, or they will atrophy.

Put on Your Track Shoes and Get Ready to Run

When I'm asked what it's like to work a shift in the E.R., I say it's like competing in a decathlon, except you have to run all ten events at the same time with no rest in between. Some faculty physicians are comfortable delegating away the sentry function. I'm not trusting enough for that. I rush from room to room, just to get an impression of each patient, to differentiate the sick from the not so sick. Fine-tuning can wait for later. In this way, no one slips through junior hands with an undetected heart attack or ruptured appendix. My goal is to have seen every patient in the E.R. before another doctor sees them, so that when I listen to their assessment, I already know if the thinking of my minions is headed in the right direction.

There are times when it's too busy for this strategy to work, particularly if I become occupied with one or two critically ill patients. Then I have to rely upon the other doctors and nurses to keep me informed about what's happening in the E.R. But the fact of the matter is that I'm in charge, and I either have to be there or have someone there who can do the job as well or better than I can.

Call it Management by walking around, Hands-on management, or whatever, but you need to put on your track shoes and get ready to run. If you sit behind a desk all day, push buttons, make phone calls, and never get in touch with the people who make your business work, they will never really learn how you think and what's important to you. They need to see you in action, not just hear how you would have managed the situation had you been there. This goes for everyone, even the CEO. Furthermore, you need to practice what you preach. If everyone else in the E.R. is busting butt and there are ten patients waiting to be seen, I don't stop and eat a five-course meal while everyone works through the lunch hour and shows total dedication to the task. If you lean on your employees to live with Saturday night stay-overs and fly cheap coach on Rocky Mountain Scareways, you'd better not be flying around on chartered jets for routine business.

Everybody Has a Bad Day

Ego has its downside. There's a natural tendency for strong-willed people to resist accepting help, particularly when someone they're trying to impress proffers it. I learned my lesson when I was a medical student trying to place an intravenous line in a young woman with a broken leg. She had a big vein, a "pipe," in her forearm that I should have been able to enter without difficulty. Unfortunately, the blood vessel rolled away from the catheter each time I stuck her skin, so I kept missing. From over my shoulder came a voice that intoned the dreaded, "Would you like me to help you with that?" It was the Senior Resident, the supervising house officer upon whose recommendation I would receive a grade.

I took his offer as a challenge, rather than a sincere offer of assistance. "No thanks, I can do it."

"Sure," he said. "If you don't mind, I'll stick around just in case you have a problem." He directed his next comment to my victim. "He's real good at this."

My determination was laced with anger. Didn't he realize he was making me nervous? I poked the poor girl twice more before she pleaded with me to let someone else try. When I looked up from her elbow and saw the tears running down her cheek, I realized what an inconsiderate wretch I had become. Just to get a grade. I hung my head and mumbled, "Could you give me a hand?"

The Senior Resident lightly traced his fingers up and down the young woman's forearm until he found precisely what he was seeking, then gently explained to her what he was going to do. With an imperceptible flick of the wrist, he slid a catheter into a vein that was invisible to me, the blessed flash of blood appeared, and the procedure was completed.

Then he showed me what it meant to have class. While he was cleaning up my mess, he thanked the patient for being such a good sport, and assured her, "You know, he's one of our best medical students. Everybody has a bad day."

Nowadays I pride myself on being able to draw blood out of a stone, but I also know that if I can't do it in one or two attempts, it's best to let someone else try. It's not a contest. It's a task and the recipient feels real pain. It may not be an ego-booster for a doctor who fails, but the patient *really* appreciates it when someone on their game gets the job done.

In the corporate suite, getting the kind of help you need presupposes that you have created an environment in which the appropriate resources exist. If you always have trouble doing your job with regularity, then you probably need to think about moving on, but when it's a bad day, let someone help. If you're the President, think what a thrill it can be for the Vice President to be rendered manifestly useful, and then praised for the effort. Don't forget the Board of Directors. It wants to know that the company is in capable hands, but sometimes its members also want to feel part of the process in a way that is contributory to problem solving.

The level of support you require as an executive depends upon your innate capabilities and how far your ego will allow you to extend in a call for help. If you're not sure how such behavior will be received, test it in small increments. Learn who helps you and then broadcasts it to the world, who considers collaborative behavior entitlement to a reward, and who assists you selflessly and out of genuine concern for the company and your welfare.

No matter how you ultimately handle a difficult situation, recognize when you're having a bad day, and try to snap out of it. The best way to convert a frustrating situation into a positive outcome is to (1) determine if the task must be completed, (2) make an honest assessment whether you need to be the person to get the job done, and (3) let someone else look good, while fulfilling the essential function and satisfying the customer. And when you ask for help, get out of the way and don't hinder your savior. If you really aren't going to hand over the reins, stay on the horse.

The Hospital Is Not a Place
Where People Wish to Be

The hospital is a very lonely place. Patients really don't wish to be there. Hospitalization implies illness, pain, suffering, separation from family and friends, unexpected expense, loss of control, and all of the other inconveniences associated with an unplanned or unavoidable period of captivity. Childbirth, cosmetic surgery, and the opportunity for healing notwithstanding, nobody wants to be in the hospital. It is most commonly a disruption of normal daily activities and a separation from whatever it is that one would rather be doing. This most essential of service businesses must struggle against the highest expectations in an enterprise that serves its customers at a time when they're most vulnerable. Talk about pressure. Multiply that tenfold in the E.R., because there's even less time to think about the amenities.

You definitely don't want your customers to feel like

they're in the hospital, or even in the doctor's office. Long waits, too much paperwork, too much expense, not enough explanations—you get it. Think about your business, particularly the service components. Your customers hate the same things—the waits, the arduous and impersonal phone tree, confusing instructions, late meals and cold food, the greeter who seems angrier than you. I could write a whole book about Burger King, Wells Fargo Bank, and Sears. How do they ever hang onto customers?

Many hospitals try to make the experience better for patients. They've tried to learn from other service industries (the pianist in the lobby came from Nordstroms), but they've also implemented solutions that could be adopted by nonhealth-care companies. Here are some of the programs that seem to work:

1. Patient advocates are people whose jobs are to advocate for the patients, not the hospital. They intervene directly on behalf of persons who can't effectively fend for themselves, which essentially is everybody that comes to the hospital. In the E.R., they most commonly come in the form of "volunteers" or "pink ladies," because if there isn't a budget for patient advocates, that's the assignment that generates the greatest amount of satisfaction.

2. Get the paperwork done in advance and include a patient profile. This is a personalization touch, not an invasion of privacy. I think that most people like to see that you

know something about them, and that there is institutional memory.

3. Consolidate the billing and get the bills out promptly. Nothing is more confusing than to receive twenty different bills for a single medical encounter, and to receive them 18 months after the event, when it's hopeless to try to reconstruct what happened. I know people who have switched providers to avoid onerous, duplicate, and tardy paperwork.

4. Monitor the behavior of anyone who fields telephone calls from customers.

5. Put hard workers in front of customers who have to stand in line to be served. How much better do you think the Department of Motor Vehicles would be if even a few of the world's slowest and least motivated civil servants were compensated on the basis of customers served per hour?

6. Make exceptions for people whenever you can if it doesn't have an appreciable impact on your bottom line. How difficult is it for me to hand a patient an extra dressing for a bandage change the next morning?

Fashion Bright Colors, Not Brown

Combination therapies can have dramatic effects. One plus one might equal four. Ingesting one type of drug to treat high blood pressure and then adding another drug that attacks the problem a different way might have a remarkable impact, compared to either therapy by itself. However, if you keep mixing in additional drugs, you get to a point of diminishing returns and then, adverse effects.

Stir red with yellow and you get orange. Blend red with blue and achieve purple. Combine green with silver and witness the brilliant Aurora Borealis. Mix yellow, red, blue, green, and silver and you get brown, which is the color of mud.

A company that specializes in hosting Internet services for hospitals is on the cutting edge. A company that coordinates medical records and distributes them efficiently on-line is ingenious. A company that provides automated disease management tools for diabetics is inspired. Each has a plan and a purpose, can be valued, and is intelligible to a Wall Street analyst. Merge the three to achieve rapid growth and you create an alligator with feathers and the central nervous system of a prairie dog. Nobody understands it, and your share price goes in the crapper.

For each business unit, and for the whole enterprise, insist on a value statement. It can be a slogan, but doesn't have to be. As a general rule, if you can't integrate value statements, you can't integrate companies. What do you get when you cross "Just Do It" with "Out of Control?" "Rewrite the Rules" with "Listen with More Intelligence?" I can count "mergers of equals" on one amputated hand. If you look carefully at the merger frenzy that accompanied the Internet mania of the last few years, the only analogy that makes sense is that of adding more paths to the rat's maze. There's still only one way out. In Boston and California, large university hospital systems combined with the rhetoric of consolidating services and controlling expenses, when the real motivation was to dominate market share. But they didn't understand the markets, and they certainly didn't know how to manage. So, instead of making things simpler, they made things more complex, adding layers of bureaucracy and never empowering the providers. Surprise, surprise, these strategies haven't worked, and literally hundreds of millions of dollars have been wasted to support the tangles created by masterminds who don't understand the culture of health care, because they've never once taken care of a patient. Major automobile manufacturers are consolidating now, but I expect that they will suffer the same fate, because the real cheerleaders for these transactions are not the workers on the line, or even the production managers, but the investment bankers who triumph on the fees and the senior managers who have parachutes modeled after lottery jackpots. Driving growth with relentless mergers is like feeding growth hormone to a giant—the end result is too tall, too heavy, and doomed to die young.

Be Serious about Your Work, but Never Take Yourself Seriously

Doctors are often characterized as having big egos. They're indoctrinated early with the importance of their profession, and sometimes confuse the significance of their calling with the significance of their personal value in the universe. While a certain amount of self-assuredness is critical to establish a sense of confidence in your patients, there can be a fine line between confidence and arrogance.

A person who is ill needs not only support, but also respect. Being sick makes you vulnerable in ways that don't occur in any other setting, regardless of the stress. No physician should practice medicine without spending time on a gurney in an E.R. looking up at the lights. It's an empty and helpless feeling to become totally dependent upon a person who possesses special knowledge, which can be difficult to share and which is often communicated in a hurried fashion. If you layer that with a condescending attitude, the patient victim can be demoralized, or worse, angered. It's all about empathy when it counts most. Medicine is special, but that doesn't entitle the practitioner to consider himself superior to his patients. That sort of deity self-image should be reserved for comparisons of physicians to attorneys.

In the helping relationship, respecting your patients and asking them to participate in their cure allow the self-dignity necessary to accept your assistance without feeling demeaned. On the other hand, treating patients as inferior only reinforces the negative stereotype of a physician as holier-than-thou and insensitive to suffering. It boils down to taking your work seriously, but not taking yourself seriously. Theoretically, we have all chosen our profession because we enjoy it and are good at it. This is not an entitlement to run roughshod over the persons we supervise, or those we care for.

It's important to distinguish a conscious effort to motivate. There are times when it becomes necessary to adopt a strict or even impatient attitude, if that's the only way to get a critical action achieved in a timely fashion. In the middle of a cardiac resuscitation, when I ask someone to stick a tube down the patient's trachea because he's stopped breathing, and the resident begins to argue about the choice of paralyzing drug or for some new approach that no one else has ever heard about, I may get a little short and say something like, "I really don't want to talk about it now—just do what I tell you!" That's not acceptable as a general teaching style, but sometimes I have to assume the mantle and keep the process moving. However, the postscript should include an unhurried educational effort, with an explanation and discussion of future options in a similar situation. If you "win" and puff out your chest, remember that it makes a bigger target for the spear that will inevitably be hurled at the leader who gloats.

Why are you running a company? If it's public, you must constantly cycle back to the mantra, "to increase shareholder value." Does that make you important? Well, it may make you feel important, but trust me; there are a lot of people who can do what you do just as well or better. So then, what would cause you to achieve longevity in a position, to be recognized as successful, or even beloved? Making the numbers is required, but isn't enough. Creating opportunities for others will take you a long way. Externally, you are creating an investment opportunity; internally, you are creating careers. Bullies create reasons for revenge; leaders create opportunities for acts of loyalty.

Stop Talking and Listen to the Patient

It's in most doctors' personalities to be assertive, to be the leaders, to try to take charge of situations. They're used to giving orders and expect people to do what's recommended for them. However, what's intended as advice often comes out as dictum. In our era of managed care, it's become even worse. Physicians now have their productivity measured by throughput of patients, which is determined by numbers rather than the quality of the experience. What should be a relaxed dialogue with a patient turns into a brief interview, rapid assessment, and abbreviated set of instructions. What gets sacrificed? The time to listen.

Other personality traits that can worsen this lack of information exchange are a desire to impress a patient and therefore to talk about oneself. Another problem is leading someone through a directed stream of dialogue in which the answers are predetermined, and the person being interviewed doesn't have the opportunity to really think about the response, or to analyze a situation in a less-than-structured response. If I ask a patient if something feels hot or cold, he will often answer "hot" when the correct answer is "it *hurts." Binary questions lead to binary thinking.*

Most people are more than willing to tell you what they think. Learning to listen is an acquired trait. Patients may not be medically sophisticated; in fact, most are not, but what they have to say is of critical importance in getting to a diagnosis or measuring the response to therapy. Even more important, one needs to appreciate the importance of listening to a person who feels vulnerable, who needs to express both the need for help and the desire to retain some autonomy for the purpose of self-respect. I cannot overemphasize the fact that the single biggest dissatisfier in the doctor-patient relationship is the perception by a patient that the doctor isn't listening, and therefore is incapable of empathy.

The only thing worse than not listening is not listening *and* smothering the person trying to communicate by talking over him. If you've heard it all before *from this person,* then you can shorten the conversation, but otherwise, it's best to hear it out. I can clearly remember a patient who had been interviewed first by a resident in training. The patient was experiencing an exacerbation of chronic heart failure, and the resident was concerned that her patient might have suffered an undetected heart attack. Multiple expensive tests were scheduled to begin the next morning. The patient was frustrated, because the resident had been in a hurry to get to the next patient and wouldn't listen to the entire story. "I wanted to tell her that I ran out of my heart pills three weeks ago and so I haven't taken any, but she was talking so fast that I forgot. I guess I was also a little embarrassed, but she was so *intimidating.*" The patient's communication to me eliminated the need for an expensive work-up for a problem that could be totally attributed to a failure to take prescribed medication. Granted, I had the benefit of being the second person to interview the patient, but I also knew that the resident was prone to being superficial, to rushing people, and to being a talker, not a listener. Furthermore, she liked to talk about herself, about what *she* needed to do, what *she* was feeling, and how each and every event affected what *her* life was like. Empathy was not in her vocabulary.

People have names, and it's important to remember them. In the E.R., where the patients turn over on the average every couple of hours, it's often difficult to memorize everyone's name. So, we're in the habit of referring to people as if they were diseases. We refer to "the gallbladder in Room 3" or "the abdominal pain in the Observation Ward." That's OK between doctors and nurses, but it's demoralizing to patients when they overhear it, because it's depersonalizing and disrespectful. I'm terrible with names, mostly because I don't pay attention during introductions. That's a real shortcoming.

Within a business unit, the people who have the greatest chance to continually ascend through leadership positions are those who listen to and clearly understand the persons for whom they are responsible. The managers who don't really listen and learn, but who feign interest in order to find an opportunity to talk and impress you with what they think, never capture the loyalties of their subordinates. I attended a monthly staff meeting in which the Office Manager allowed everyone to speak briefly, only to interrupt them or follow immediately with her interpretation of what had been presented, or a frank comment that the important point had been missed. Not only had she not been listening, but she violated each speaker's sense of self-worth. It was an example of horrible micromanagement. Although it wasn't ill intentioned, it portrayed insecurity and disregard for the feelings of others that absolutely precluded my considering her for additional responsibilities. It's better to remain silent than to say nothing.

The Patient Is Sick, Not You

A doctor's bedside manner is his most powerful public relations tool. Despite that fact, how many times have you heard someone say, "He's got a horrible bedside manner," then continue about how they allow that physician to continue to care for them. They may even profess to love the doctor. That's the power of the doctor-patient relationship. Maybe a better explanation is that the patient has no better alternative.

Doctors can do and say some pretty insensitive things. Being a doctor myself, I know that some of these lapses in interpersonal communication are spoken in jest, are ill-timed truths, or are signs of frustration. The dumbest comment is, "I've got it worse than you." While this may be true, the patient is paying you (or someone) to be sympathetic, not hard-hearted. It's all right to be judgmental, like when you tell a smoker to quit, and in certain circumstances it's OK to share your own experiences with a patient if these are instructive or motivational. But it's not a doctor's place to decide that he's worse off than the patient, and to use that as a lever of reprimand or guilt. Even though I've worked through shifts in the E.R. while suffering my own physical ailments, that's my problem, not yours.

If someone walks into your office whining about how horrible they've got it, make a noncomparative evaluation of the merit of the complaint. Judged against whatever is proper, is their beef legitimate? Don't make your decision based on what you feel should be your circumstances (and how they compare with the other person's), or measure their expectations against your personal frustrations, because then you might decide that nobody is entitled to be happy. If you're an impaired physician or business leader, does that mean that everybody has to be more miserable than you to get any attention?

I've watched physicians withhold pain medications from patients with broken bones because when they had *their* broken legs, they "toughed it out." That's a real relationship builder. Patients who are overweight and out of shape may be considered with disdain by doctors who are athletes. These physicians mistake the bully pulpit to which they are entitled, which is in the field of medicine, for a soapbox upon which they promulgate their personal beliefs about lifestyle, religion, and politics.

You're a business leader, and need to avoid role-playing a parent, preacher, or law enforcement officer. If you want sympathy, see the doctor, not the VP of Business Development. If someone comes to you for routine advice, and goes away feeling like they should be burned at the stake, you need to go to charm school.

Nobody Lies on His Deathbed and Says, "I Wish I Had Spent More Time at the Office"

My first patient one morning was a hard-driving executive in a venture capital firm. He was suffering excruciating chest pain. He lived out of airports and prided himself on two facts—first, that he had been home twice in the past month, and second, that he was finally getting to know his teenaged sons. He'd been to thirteen cities in five days. He said that the financial rewards of his position were "great" and that he would "reap millions" from the deals he had done. As he was having his heart attack and I whipped him off to the cardiac care unit to undergo an angioplasty, I hoped that he would make it to see tomorrow's sunrise.

Your body is the great leveler. Everyone's on the same playing field when they get sick, especially if it's something bad like a heart attack or cancer. Working in the E.R., one acquires an overwhelming appreciation for

93

how quickly it can all end, and how often the terminal event was precipitated by behaviors that were totally unnecessary. Drunk drivers are the most obvious and horrific. *Less blatant are the workaholics, who pretend to thrive on stress right up to the moment when they drop dead.* Doctors are some of the worst offenders, because their indoctrination from day one is that they're expected to be stoic and uncomplaining, and to accept any workload without complaint.

In the absence of luck and even with truly great talent, most of us need to work hard to become high achievers. There's nothing wrong with that. Productivity, a sense of responsibility, lofty goals, and personal pride lead sensible and balanced individuals to approach their work aggressively, even with passion. However, there comes a point of diminishing returns. Fatigue leads to poor judgment and sloppy work, and chronic fatigue leads to burnout. Stress in all forms is cumulative. Emergency physicians are notorious for working to exhaustion, and so they eventually seek a less stressful environment. It shouldn't be the graveyard.

The warning signs should be obvious to any manager. Apathy, mood swings, tardiness, lack of attention to detail, an uncaring or negative attitude, late assignments, crude comments, unfriendliness, and error-prone behavior should raise the red flag. When physical ailments include frequent headaches, decreasing appetite, difficulty sleeping, abdominal cramps, hyperventilation, and chest discomfort, it's possible that stress is leading to physical and social impairments. The first step to intervention is recognition that there's a problem.

For the macho leader, perhaps someone "without a life," stressed behavior in others may be considered a sign of weakness. In some circumstances, it certainly can be. However, no manager should be so crass as to ignore his responsibility in a situation when stressed behavior is eroding a person or the business. In that situation, it's the manager's job to step in and either remove the stress, support the individual who is having problems, or find another solution before a critical deficiency or error occurs. The time-honored solution is teamwork, but sometimes that's not practical. Still, don't be overly harsh in your response to those who need your help, unless they are absolutely resistant to advice or change. There's an art form to being a coach when someone is struggling, and knowing when to offer suggestions rather than issue orders. When you get "push-back" and didn't realize you were pushing, evaluate your accountability for creating a stressful environment.

Use Metrics That Make Sense

The jury is out on whether or not managed care will lower health-care costs, but there's no question that it introduced a metronome into medicine. Time is the one measurement that everyone can follow for which there is a common unit. Satisfaction is often difficult to measure and subject to great debate, so productivity for physicians has been conveniently translated into the number of patients they can see each hour and the cost per patient. Does this make sense? If you're paying for piecework, it does. It forces physicians and their staffs to examine each segment of the care delivery process and to eliminate the inefficiencies, but taken to the extreme, it strips out all of the niceties. Handholding doesn't save lives, but it takes time, so it disappears.

For sure, there are benefits to holding health-care providers accountable for productivity. So, at what price have we saved money? At the price of less personal choice, discouraged doctors, burned-out nurses, and patients who find it necessary to seek protection with legislation that preserves their rights. Lest I be accused of being another complaining practitioner, let me state that I recognize that these issues are complex, and that a fee-for-service, cost-plus medical system has flaws, including overutilization and the potential for fraud and abuse. However, that's not the point. The issue here is that the measurements, or metrics, used to determine the effectiveness of a program can take on a life of their own, and may do just as much to depress as to inspire the subjects. Doctors don't want to be measured like robots on an assembly line, and patients, although they hate to wait, don't want to be rushed.

Let's imagine you're introducing a program where the expectations are brand new. You need to have a way to determine effectiveness, other than general impressions, so you require something to observe, or score, or measure. When you cook something, you care about how it looks, smells, and tastes. There is no implied offense with the method of measurement. One can argue about the subjectivity of the process, but not that you are evaluating the wrong parameters.

Now let's consider the health-care example. Even though all of the changes you wish to make can be aggregated into a simple measure of number of patients per hour, just the very thought of it is frequently offensive to people who consider their work an art, not a mechanical function. Maybe they are wrong and need to have their thinking converted, but you won't accomplish this by slapping them in the face. Remember that the most precious commodities you have as a manager are your thought leaders. So, while it's useful to point out how process changes contribute to efficiency, which can be measured as improvements in throughput time, perhaps a more constructive approach would be to measure patient satisfaction, better staffing ratios that free up precious resources for other critical tasks, and new programs generated out of the savings. Of course, if all you are about is saving money (euphemistically pawned off as "operations improvements"), then you won't like this approach.

For a new project, take your vision and mold it into a desired outcome. Break it down into incremental steps that represent progress, and figure out how you will know if you get there. What is the benefit for the actors, and what is the benefit for the audience? Do they feel it, or can they measure it? If you were going to market your new program, what metric would you find most effective from a sales perspective? Would it be general or specific? Would the measures you chose to gauge your effectiveness be supportive in and of themselves, or would they elicit negative feelings and pushback? Can you link a reward to a laudable measure of progress? Can the process itself, rather than the outcome, become the carrot? Never underestimate the effect of a disappointing grade upon someone who is looking for a subtle positive stroke, not a black-and-white rating that seems final and potentially embarrassing.

Inspire Confidence, Not Fear

As in any other corporate setting, there's a hierarchy in medicine. This is magnified in an academic setting, wherein resides the pomp and pageantry of the Dean, the academic Chairs, the trustees, and all of the donors and privileged people who determine the fate of the medical center. The bureaucracy often multiplies at the expense of development at the "troops" level, and many in developing roles envy those who have attained positions of power.

There are many ways to lead, some wonderful and creative, and some hideous and inhibitory. As one Surgery Department Chairman taught me early on, he could get his Chief Resident to do anything he ordered through intimidation, but he would engender very little loyalty.

On the other hand, if he took the time to instill confidence in his residents, they would follow him to the end of the earth (and put up with an ungodly amount of work).

True leaders create other leaders, and in the process have the easiest path to the formation of a team. Simplified, this means that if you are intent upon teaching and observation of your students, and in the process constantly search for leaders, then you will have the best chance to perform an accurate assessment of each and every person you observe. The manager who blindly operates off the organization chart without having sufficient knowledge of key individuals is doomed to unpleasant surprises, which usually come at the worst possible moments.

In order for people to learn and become inspired, they need role models. Internal drive, or "fire in the belly," is enviable but extraordinary. Most people need to be nurtured, rather than stoked. It's traditional in much of medical teaching to let students, and then residents, fly on their own, to put them in charge of extremely ill patients and then offer remarkably little support. The theory is that one learns by doing, and that near-mistakes have intrinsic teaching value that justifies the risk to patients.

Two episodes, one positive and one negative, that occurred early in my medical training had enormous influence over my attitude toward medicine and teaching. In the first, I was a medical student assigned to the internal medicine ward. I accepted a particularly complex patient with a confusing clinical presentation. As part of the evaluation, I was required to perform a "lupus prep," taking hours to prepare a glass slide with a blood smear from the patient, stained to highlight a particular type of blood cell supposedly diagnostic for the disease systemic lupus erythematosus. The preparation was arduous, I was alone without supervision, and I kept making mistakes, ruining slide after slide. At two in the morning and having been on the wards for eighteen hours, I was tired, cranky, and without motivation. Just as I was about to throw in the towel, a firm hand gripped my shoulder and a stern voice demanded, "Let me see what you've got there."

I turned around prepared to curse and stared straight into the face of the most famous Emeritus Professor in America, who still roamed the hospital as an unpaid volunteer at all hours in search of young doctors to teach and patients to benefit. He looked into the microscope, observed my inadequate stain, and shook his head. I was prepared to be humbled. However, instead of using his superior intellect to intimidate me, he said matter-of-factly, "Move over," methodically prepared a slide, and then showed me what I had been searching for—a "lupus cell." He then instructed me to follow his example and coached me to success in completing a task that, to this day, I have never again attempted. When I thanked him, he shrugged his shoulders and said, "You'll be a doctor."

The second example was less satisfying. Prior to being allowed to start clinical rotations, I took a course entitled "Physical Diagnosis" to learn the art of interviewing and examining patients. I was assigned to take a history and complete a physical examination of a man with suspected cirrhosis of the liver. When I entered his room, he had just returned from enduring a liver biopsy, which entailed insertion of a hollow needle through his abdominal wall into his liver in order to procure a piece of that organ for microscopic examination. He wore a large bandage over his abdomen, and the skin surrounding the gauze was still painted orange and carried the smell of antiseptic.

I asked him many questions. Despite his discomfort, he was extremely cooperative. I instructed him to stand up and walk around the room, then pressed on his abdomen and had him cough, strain, and otherwise perturb his postbiopsy recovery period. He seemed tired, but none the worse for the wear. I thanked him, left his room, and walked to the doctors' charting area to record my observations.

A few minutes later, a furious young doctor stood at the nursing station and yelled, "Who examined the patient with the liver biopsy? Who was the *idiot* who examined him?"

My heart dropped into my stomach. I began to sweat. "I did."

"You moron. You probably killed him! Don't you know that he's supposed to be absolutely still for six hours after a biopsy? He's probably bleeding to death right now! You get your ass in there."

The resident was right about the prohibition, but the patient seemed all right. Still, what did I know? I wasn't a doctor. No one had told me. I was frightened beyond comprehension. This was my first patient, and now he might die because of me! I didn't know what else to do, and I didn't have anywhere to turn, so I sat in that room for the next six hours with my hand on the patient's wrist, taking his pulse and asking him every five minutes if he was OK. He just wanted to go to sleep and begged me to leave, but I wouldn't go.

Later, I called my physical diagnosis instructor. He laughed and told me that I had been reprimanded by a resident with a reputation for being hard on the medical students and that I shouldn't take it to heart. In all honesty, I have to say that the episode will always stay with me as an example of how to turn a great teaching opportunity into a horrible experience. Had my error been pointed out to me in a civil fashion, I would have been just as mortified at what I had done, but wouldn't have been humiliated. Later in the week, I apologized to the resident, then told him that if he ever treated me that way again, we'd settle it outside. He had been right, but he was a jerk. I was now his enemy. If he had used his head instead of his ego, he might have had a loyal subject.

If All You Ever Needed to Know You Learned in Kindergarten, You'll Kill a Lot of Patients

Everybody loves a good slogan, but don't overdo it. I think that people get more inspiration from how you behave than from a picture of an eagle soaring over the

Grand Canyon with an inscription about religion, team-work, and making your dreams come true.

Some people believe that a person learns everything they really need to know in kindergarten. You know—truth, loyalty, compassion, sharing, friendship, sports-manship, love, flowers, puppies, snowflakes, toilet training, and the tooth fairy. I think the most important thing I learned in kindergarten was which end of my milk carton to open. Not discounting the "soft side" of what we do in medicine, and how important it is to truly care for people, if all I ever needed to know I learned in kindergarten, then my patients would be in big trouble. They may love me or hate me for how I hold their hand or show them respect, but they live or die depending on how well I can read an x-ray or stitch a wound. A complete healer attends to the bodies and souls of his patients, but if I had to choose between one or the other, I'd take the doctor who knew what to do with my body.

I'm usually the first to comment that one can never underestimate the value of "human resources." By this, I do not mean the precise administration of benefits plans, parking stickers, and employee assistance pro-grams. These are necessities that even the most callous manager can't ignore. What I mean by human resources is the complete development of all aspects of your employees, to address both their technical skills and how these are properly applied in an environment predicated upon human interaction. This is adult education. A paint mixer who never has to do anything but push buttons and measure shades of orange doesn't need to undergo training in customer service, but the person at the front desk who answers the phone is your front line and needs to know everything about how sick people think and feel. The people skills become technical requirements for performance and should be measured, or at least commented upon with regularity. However, you can overdo it and end up with a company of schmoozers who are so intent upon the emotional responses of their peers that they forget the identity of their primary customers. Work is supposed to be pleasant and productive, but it isn't supposed to be primal therapy or a substitute for a healthy home environment. Chanting and aromatherapy are great diversions, but if you need a special program in the workplace to generate stress reduction, wouldn't it make more sense to get at the first cause, and seek to lower the inherent level of stress? My personal opinion is that people who are insecure or guilt-ridden are often the most stressed. If they're doing a good job, the guilt usually has something to do with a work-home imbalance. If they're not doing a good job, then they're insecure, and you should either work to bring them up to par or find something else for them to do. The solution usually centers primarily on the technical aspects of the job, and then on the touchy-feely stuff. A pleasant work environment and collegial relationships are strengthened by competence.

Golden Handcuffs Are Not Enough

There are many component parts to a busy academic E.R., each of which requires leadership: the clinical practice, business administration, resident training, academic policies, and research. Subsets that require additional expertise are community relations, marketing, nursing practice, prehospital care, equipment and supplies, pharmacy policy, medical student teaching, and sometimes poison center, trauma center, and aeromedical transport.

It's the rare person who can optimally manage all of these elements. So, the Chief of Emergency Medicine assigns different roles to the faculty, each of whom is expected to be a superb clinician in addition to being an effective leader in his or her special area. The Chief conducts this symphony from a score written by the university, medical center, and local community. Because emergency medicine is a relatively young specialty, there are many opportunities for leadership, and not enough good people to fill them. The talented individuals migrate to these opportunities quickly, because they're motivated and because they are very much needed. Therefore, the brain drain is significant. It's unrealistic to expect to hold onto midlevel managers without a sequence of regular promotions or unless you have golden handcuffs, and I would contend that even these incentives are rarely enough.

I've always done my best to retain the best people as long as I could, but that doesn't match up particularly well with "Surround Yourself with the Best People You Can and Work Hard to Make Them Look Good." If people have ambition, when they begin to look really good, their motivation causes them to move on. If you care about their careers, as you expected others to care for your career, then you're obligated to do well by them, which means helping them get ahead. Now you have created a void, and the process begins all over again.

Your only method for countering the maturation and eventual departure of home-grown leaders is to continually teach, train, harvest, and recruit. That is the single most important role for senior management. An organization that's not in continual renewal at its senior and midmanagement levels is ill fated, sooner or later, because it's vulnerable to the abilities of recruiters, who have a predictable failure rate. I'm not advocating inbreeding, because you don't have to start the maturation process at the entry level and hope to develop your next CEO. A much more sensible approach is to drop down two levels on the organization chart and see from where you are likely to promote in order to maintain equilibrium at the top. In the E.R., it's most natural to become the Chief from the Associate Chief or Clinical Director positions, because these are the positions most akin to Vice President. To encourage the recruitment of new blood, one would develop a cycle of recruiting or training into one or both of these positions, see how things work out, and be developing the next Chief, who might or might not stay, depending on how long the delay is to ascend. In your company, you should always have a plan for your next generation of leadership, and educate into it.

Sometimes Having to Keep Secrets Is Necessary

I'm certain that what I'm about to say next will offend some patient advocates who believe that every patient should participate in each decision made in the course of their care. Such a philosophical position requires that the patient know everything that can reasonably be explained to them, for how else is one to be sufficiently informed in order to make a critical decision?

Sometimes this isn't possible, other times it isn't necessary, and occasionally it is ill advised. Believe it or not, sometimes it's correct to address a patient and family and with the straightest of faces proclaim a half-truth, or even what most people would consider an out and out lie. This is done not to deceive, but to maintain a position of hope, which is as important for the healer as it is for the patient. A cold recitation of the odds of survival, the chance for a deformity, or the short number of days left to live meet the requirements for telling the truth, but rarely offer solace when a person is crying out for a reason to live or to find a way to cope with a horrible situation.

So, I do it. And unless they are unfeeling automatons, so do other physicians. We're not pathological liars, just doctors trying to finesse our way through situations of emotional complexity far beyond a shipment of semiconductors or publication of a marketing piece. We withhold the absolute, precious information with trepidation and a great deal of unease, but we do it anyway, because it is simply the right thing to do. I know that whenever I hold back the details or twist a story to make it better than it is, I am uncomfortable and bear a double burden—that of being a liar and that of now having to decide when to change the story. Sooner or later, dreadfully ill patients sense one of two things—either that they feel too awful to be doing as well as I say they're doing, or that I am uncomfortable, and must be holding out on something. It's a burden to not be truthful, but part of every doctor's liability.

Another situation that leads to less than forthright behavior arises in the role of educator, when it becomes necessary to let the hopelessly failing medical student begin to understand that he or she will never make it as a doctor. This is a rare communication that is undertaken with the utmost trepidation, but someone has to make the call.

In business, one lies to gain time or perhaps to let someone down easy, but the act of not telling the truth creates the same burden and risk. "The check's in the mail" is a good example of the former. Is it correct to make such a statement if this is an untruth? Probably not, because the gain is all for one's self, not for the benefit of another. It's simply not the same to pretend to be on time as it is to hold back on personal bad news in the attempt to maintain hope. Getting caught in a personal lie designed to protect your business unit carries grave consequences, like those bestowed upon a company in the public marketplace that does not meet financial expectations. Of course, in that case, the lie may first have been created by the analysts, who then punish the company for not delivering upon their fantasy. To paraphrase Kurt Vonnegut, you are what you pretend to be, so you need to be careful about what you pretend to be.

Cushioning the painful truth from someone who is likely to suffer at your appraisal is noble and may or may not be the right thing to do, just like withholding the truth from a patient may or may not be right. Remember, though, the charade cannot go on forever. Much like children in a schoolyard, co-workers tend to be interpersonally cruel when they sense weakness, and will expose the managerial mollycoddler long before the executive leadership spots any favoritism. This is often couched in the rubric of fairness, but I believe has more to do with what some might perceive as an unfair advantage.

I have lied as a business leader in an effort to allow an individual to act without the pressure of my criticisms, which can be intense. In other words, I have in essence tried to intentionally commend someone for a job well done, highlighting the positive, when I really felt that someone was a misfit, doomed to failure. As often as I have tried this method, it has failed, because the tormented individuals contrive self-abusive patterns that cannot be eradicated by simple acts of kindness. They need to be managed within a structure that limits their ability to inflict negativism upon others. So, I usually cycle back to sitting down with the underachiever, laying it all on the line and letting future behavior speak for the response.

Never Become Complacent, Because Advantage Is Temporary

When a person suffers a severe blow to the head, one of the significant arteries to the brain can be torn. If this occurs, the bleeding may create an expanding blood clot that produces a syndrome known as an "epidural" (outside the covering of the brain) "hematoma" (blood clot). The classic medical story describes a victim who was knocked unconscious, awoke with a headache, appeared to do well for an hour or two, and then abruptly lapsed into a coma. With this neurosurgical catastrophe, there has to be an immediate life-saving operation. So, an emergency physician caring for a head-injured patient can never become complacent.

Any sense of security in business is a false sense of security. We all hope to dominate our competitors, to gain advantage and keep it. Things look better, then they look worse. On Monday, a biotechnology stock is a high-flier, and on Tuesday, a Wall Street analyst says it's oversold and the price plummets. What happened? The company is no different; it's just that the momentum is gone. A physician practice management company holds contracts to operate a hundred E.R.'s, and then a hospital chain switches to another management company because of some irrelevant (to the E.R. business) political consideration. There was no problem with service, no problem with the doctors. What happened?

As nature abhors a vacuum, businesses abhor stability. It's been suggested that only the paranoid survive. Perhaps paranoia is too strong a term, but complacency is the polar opposite and a guaranteed way to get into trouble. Your competitors will take your business any way they can. If it can't be earned, it will be stolen, and if you look foolish in the process, all the better, because that will make it more difficult for you to win the business back.

The reason I used the epidural hematoma example was to make the point of pattern recognition. Most of the problems you encounter that lead to lost business, a crisis of consumer confidence, or some other business problem are part of recurrent themes, for which any competent manager should be prepared. Let me perseverate. You can't just wait for these things to happen. You have to be on top of the likely situations that might go bad, and work proactively to root them out and fix any problems before they become irrevocable. *When your customer calls in a consultant to offer advice about a service for which you are responsible, you can kiss the business good-bye.* If you're fortunate enough to get a lucid interval between a blow to the head and the eruption from a torn blood vessel, you'd better have gotten to a diagnosis, found a solution, and begun to apply it.

Paul S. Auerbach, M.D.

When there's a real issue of product integrity, you should clear the shelves and calm your customers, but proclaim your innocence *only* after you have the facts. I understand that the law says that you are innocent until proven guilty, but this is not judicial advice. When I get a complaint about any aspect of a doctor's performance, I'm immediately all over it, because the stakes are so high. The health and safety of patients, personal reputation of the doctor, image of the E.R., status of the medical center, exposure to civil and criminal liability—these can all precipitate from a seemingly minor incident. I serve notice immediately to my customer and to my employee, both of whom are my responsibility, that this has the highest priority. I never try to minimize what a complaint might mean, but at the same time, I keep my fact finding private and off the record, until I know what I am dealing with. When I get a letter of praise about a doctor's performance, I feel no less compelled to act, but a round of applause is not as time-critical as a sigh of relief.

Let Your People Know What Makes You Angry

The same way that children are sensitive to their parents, patients are sensitive to their doctors. Moody physicians have a difficult time gaining loyalty, because what patients expect are a sensitive approach and constant good humor. Of course, practicing medicine is often extremely emotional, and there are many reasons for a health-care professional to be discouraged, disappointed, exhausted, or angry. However, staff or patients do not appreciate a show of "low" emotions. It is a measure of high esteem, but probably unrealistically high expectations, that leads patients to be saddened and confused by healers who are impatient or disgruntled.

I try not to get angry with patients, but it happens. In the E.R., a doctor from time to time gets insulted, slapped, or spit upon. Anger is the appropriate human response, but it gets restrained, by custom and by policy. The law supports self-defense, but it isn't good marketing to hit the patients.

However, with one's co-workers, it's a different dynamic. Here, expectations may run just as high on both sides. That is, the nurses and technicians lose their equilibrium when the doctors lose their temper. Yelling and screaming are not effective leadership techniques in a health-care environment, and always come off as petulance of the overprivileged. A stern look and quiet approach to discipline are much more effective, reserving demands, rank, and force for the most critical situations, when time is of the essence and persuasion is an ill-afforded luxury.

The preventive solution to anger is avoidance. Sometimes a person will do something so stupid, inadequate, disrespectful, or illogical that anger wells up uncontrollably; in at least half of these circumstances, there were no limits or previously defined expectations for the offender. Most health-care professionals aren't idiots, but they still need guidance and guidelines for behavior and performance. The medical student who refused to see the patient without insurance had never been told that we see everybody, regardless of their ability to pay; the intern who wouldn't allow the child's mother to accompany him into the intensive care unit had never been oriented to hospital policy. Most people aren't clairvoyant, particularly in a situation where there are multiple leaders. In the midst of complexity and egos, you will gain loyalty by explaining first and shouting later, rather than vice versa.

Stepping into a new senior management role, particularly if it is operational and you are new to the organization, is fraught with risk. Change is difficult, and employees are fearful that you will bring a new approach that exceeds their capability to adapt or which they just don't like. They want your attention, or even affection, but cannot fully invest themselves in you emotionally as a leader until they're convinced that you'll be around for a while. This is the critical time at which to spend adequate time to make clear your goals and expectations for performance, to emphasize rules you wish to promote, and to let everyone understand what makes you angry. Try to do it in a way that invites your listeners to see you as a resource, rather than a scorekeeper, and use examples.

Achieve for Your Children, Not for Your Mother

My mother always encouraged me to be a doctor. This statement has more relevance than most people ever imagine. We are in large part a product of our upbringing, driven by some level of desire to achieve for someone or something. We may measure our accomplishments in the praise and accolades we receive from others, often neglecting the internal sense of satisfaction that might be a healthier measure of performance.

In medicine, there is a present and a future. The past is irrelevant, except for the historical aspects that frame predictions of the future. The reasons why physicians dwell so obsessively on the history of a patient or an illness is to gather clues to come to a diagnosis, not to draw general inferences that lead to lessons of value for a general population. Preventive medicine is the closest the medical profession comes to planning, but it's far too primitive at this point to be useful, in part because individual preferences and opinions supersede the premise that anything uniform can be implemented to affect general behaviors and health. Screening for diseases is useful when the benefits of discovery outweigh the risks and costs of the tests. However, it takes self-motivation on the part of individuals to adhere to a healthy lifestyle or to abandon bad habits.

In business, patterns of prior behavior are more useful, because managers are trained to be aggressive when they spot tendencies that expose problems or that might lead to opportunities. We study trends and seize a chance to dominate a market, which as a business principle can apply to medicine, but isn't of as much value in directing a scientific effort.

Paul S. Auerbach, M.D.

For whom is the effort made? In part, to please our superiors. This crosses over all professions and isn't unique to business or medicine. Customer satisfaction is an immediate strategy and helps keep us all employed. It's valuable insofar as it implies that somebody's needs are being met, but it doesn't necessarily imply long-term value in any sort of creative sense. Whether you land a customer or set a broken bone, you have done something appropriate and good, and your mother is happy, but what is the benefit to your children?

Research is future-directed. Legislative programs that diminish tobacco consumption leave a legacy that will have a positive impact on future generations. Finding a cure for a disease makes the world better for those that will follow, even if it's not in time to help those who are currently suffering.

The parallel in business is investment in methods that can reform the way a business feels, thinks, and moves. It's the willingness to challenge assumptions, to advance the science of an industry, or to deploy the workforce in a way that creates opportunities for future workers to follow. As you decide how to go forward, ask how what you are doing will benefit your children. If you add a new product line, does it enable growth within an industry or lead logically to more ideas that will enable progress? If you can articulate a way in which your proposal will go beyond making money and be genuinely useful to society, even to your children, then there might be something truly special to what you have devised. If, on the other hand, you have generated a purely financial manipulation, or your next acquisition will be taped to a limb of your organization headed for an amputation, then your "innovation" will not have sustained value.

Stay Well Hydrated

Three experiences come to mind. When I was an intern, the most grueling rotation was a month in the intensive care units. This involved caring for patients in both the medical ICU and the cardiac care unit. Because it was autumn in New England, both units were full to capacity because many of the patients were elders who rode the buses into New Hampshire and Vermont to view the fall colors, only to collapse. There were only two interns at a time on this assignment, so I was on call every other night. This translated into a pattern of 36 hours in the hospital, then 12 off, with the working hours often being 40 hours straight interspersed with only 8 hours off, in order to accommodate the workload. This meant that you worked for 40 consecutive hours without sleep, then had a few hours to go home, eat, collapse, and get ready for the next work cycle. Over the course of the month, the fatigue factor was cumulative, made worse by having to care constantly for persons suffering from heart attacks, strokes, severe infections, kidney failure, and the like. I remember more than one night when two or three patients suffered cardiac arrests and died. That's how sick everybody was.

The service was grueling, and took each young doctor to his or her personal physical and emotional limits. There were tales of breakdowns. I can remember nights when I was so tired that I honestly didn't care whether patients lived or died—I just wanted to get some sleep. The quicker a cardiac arrest ended, the sooner you could get back to the call room and jump in a bunk.

Did we make bad decisions because we were so tired? Did we question our ability to cope? Did we develop a callous attitude and resentment toward the system? You bet. The stronger interns tried to thrive in that environment, but in the end, no one could sustain the energy level that would have made us sharp and maximally effective. Fortunately for the patients and the doctors, times have changed and these sorts of schedules have largely been replaced with a more sensible approach. However, with declining resources and tighter budgets in health care, I suspect we will see "the old days" creep back into medicine. The macho taskmasters will always exist, regardless of the finances.

Bad habits die hard. When I became a faculty member and then Chief of an academic E.R., I made the rules and approved the schedule. While I understood lightening up the workload for the trainees, I was less sympathetic with the faculty and even harder on myself. I began to lose track of the hours and the toll of the effort, and tasked myself in an ever-increasing spiral. One blatant episode of self-abuse provided my own personal wake-up call.

I had been working 14-hour days and not paying much attention to sleep, meals, or recreation. I was becoming increasingly tired and dehydrated. After a particularly busy day seeing patients in the E.R., which began at dawn and went on well into the evening, I went home feeling a bit ill and sick to my stomach. That brief flash of nausea was all it took to set off a wicked physiological reaction. My vagus nerve, the neural bundle that normally controls (slows down) a person's heart rate, was stimulated and caused my heart rate to drop from a normal rate of 55 beats per minute to around 25. At that rate, my heart couldn't pump enough blood to my brain to keep me conscious, so I passed out. Fatigue and dehydration kept my body from compensating, so although I had a few moments when my heart rate sped up enough for me to be barely conscious, I kept blacking out. My wife called a friend for help. They loaded me in the back of a car and I ended up back in the same E.R. where I had just finished the day as the doctor in charge!

The staff was extremely upset when they saw their new chief hauled in unconscious with a heart problem. They acted swiftly and aggressively. I was given drugs to accelerate my heart rate and quell my nausea, and intravenous fluids to replenish my cells. Over the next 8 hours, I was returned to the land of the living.

Did I learn from this lesson? Not right away. In the morning, I signed myself out of the E.R. to board a flight from San Francisco to Chicago for a meeting. I looked like death warmed over and sat through the meeting like a zombie, accomplishing nothing except to restart the cycle of overextension. Flying back home and feeling ultimately wrung out, I reflected on my stupidity. I was young and relatively healthy, so my body could tolerate an occasional assault. I vowed to drink lots of water and for a while, sought balance between exertion and rest.

Six years later, now in the role of COO of a public company, the same thing happened to me, except this time I was sitting in a ski lift chair when stress, lack of sleep, altitude, and dehydration all conspired to render me unconscious. If I hadn't smacked my companion in the head with a ski pole as I slumped down in the lift chair, he wouldn't have grabbed me and I would have fallen to an untimely end. I remember the worried look on the faces of the Ski Patrol as they bundled me up in a sled and raced me down the hill. Another round of medicine and I.V. hydration and another embarrassing moment of total vulnerability. *I am not invincible. The fire in my belly can incinerate me.*

Your drive and enthusiasm may know no bounds, but the body has limits. Not only must you respect this for yourself, but you absolutely must respect this for your employees. We often exhort our people to work "until the job gets done," to "do whatever it takes," to "go hard now and take a break later." There isn't much difference between the football coach who goes full pads and two-a-days in 90-degree heat at the beginning of the season and the CEO who requires his staff to work weekends and late into the evenings on a regular basis. Both are demoralizing, exhausting, and potentially injurious. No work environment should be designed to be exploitative. The human requirements for balance, rest, and good health must be met, or in the long run, the enterprise will fail, because good people will leave or keel over.

As far as leadership goes, show good judgment. If you can't gauge your own fuel tank, then appoint a watchdog to let you know when you're running out of gas. If you push yourself to the limit all the time and have no reserves, then when you really need a superhuman effort, it just won't be there. It's amazing how much better you will function when you get a little exercise, get enough sleep, and don't skip meals. Now when I walk into the E.R., I carry a bottle of Gatorade and drink it all down.

A Cure in Search of a Disease Is Like a Business in Search of a Revenue Model

You may be able to sell the future, but you have to deliver the present. If I asked anyone in the medical profession what that meant, they would immediately respond, "information technology." It is the most obvious area for improvement in health care, yet has been the most difficult to implement.

The most common reason why patients seek care in the E.R. is because they are in pain. The health-care system at large is a nine-to-five, Monday-through-Friday operation that simply cannot accommodate all the needs

Paul S. Auerbach, M.D.

of those who become acutely ill. If you've ever had a toothache and tried to find a dentist after hours or on a weekend, you know what I mean.

For the truly suffering, pain relief is an immediate matter. Promises of a root canal or tooth extraction at some point in the future are important, but not as much as a shot right now, because my tooth is killing me! While you are scheduling my appointment, *please* give me something for the pain. When it stops hurting, I can focus on what I need to do to attain a more definitive, long-term cure.

I hope the I.T. professionals are paying attention. I look forward to the day when a national electronic medical record will perfect confidentiality and efficient transfer of medical information; when a business-to-business application services provider will enable me to order medical supplies at the deepest discounts; and when artificial intelligence will guide me to a precise diagnosis. However, I've been listening to these solutions for years. I know I need a new crown, but could you please make it stop hurting first? You just sold me four new programs for my Palm Pilot, and convinced me to go wireless. But where are some phones that work?

I'm betting on the simple solutions that provide genuine analgesia for the business pain that everyone suffers. Information technology that is predicated on what we will do *next* really doesn't help me solve the problems I have *today*. I think that all I.T. vendors should be paid on performance, plain and simple. If I have information or process "pain," and your I.T. analgesic doesn't make me feel any better, why should I pay for it? As a manager, drive a hard bargain and make your I.T. vendors back up future claims with today's performance.

Take Time to Explain Everything

Patients sue doctors for two reasons: there's been an adverse outcome or the doctor has a bad relationship with the patient. Either situation is made worse when the doctor's been a poor communicator. If the doctor is arrogant or adversarial, it throws fuel on the fire. Perhaps the doctor and the patient have even become enemies.

To satisfy people who depend upon you or who are trying to learn from you, you *must* take your time, be certain that your audience is not distracted and capable of listening, offer information at an appropriate educational level, and gather feedback so that you can be certain that your message has been understood.

It's a hurry-up world. In medicine in particular, everyone wants to cut costs. Since time is money and fewer minutes with a patient make *somebody* wealthier, whatever isn't absolutely necessary becomes a distraction and an unwelcome expense. The casualties are time, touch, and kindness. As more and more physicians are judged on their productivity (number of patients seen) and as the staff that supports them dwindles in numbers, fewer minutes are available to simply sit and explain things. This is a horrible turn of events, because it ruins the doctor-patient relationship and leads to misunderstandings—a situation of real or perceived neglect. After all, patients want (and need) to be cared for, not become parts of some production process.

This is a conundrum, because you can only spread a doctor so thin. A lot of noncritical information can be relayed in written format, transmitted by the nurses and technicians, and even displayed on the Internet. However, when you don't feel good, and particularly when the news is bad, there's no substitute for having your doctor sit beside you, hold your hand, look you straight in the eye, and take the time to *communicate* with you.

In this regard, the art of management is not different from the art of medicine. If you run your business by cranking out memos, break important news in large impersonal gatherings or by e-mail, and delegate the difficult interpersonal messages to your assistants, then you might as well be a robot, and your employees will rightfully resent you. This doesn't mean that you have to sing Happy Birthday or wear your heart on your sleeve. Rather, it means that there are a minimum amount of time and certain key situations in your business during and for which you must be the messenger. *If you are the glue that holds your organization together, you must ooze down into every crack, and there's no better way to do this than by talking to people.*

It's an axiom in the E.R. that you can't perform a reliable examination of someone's spine if they have a painful injury in another body region. The distraction from a bad burn or mangled foot can easily supersede the perception of pain from an injured bone in the neck. So, if someone comes in after an accident in which the mechanism of injury was sufficient to break her neck and she's distracted by another injury, isn't fully conscious, is impaired by drugs or alcohol, or is incoherent, then it requires a set of x-rays to rule out a fractured spine.

The same holds true when you have an important conversation with someone for whom there is a crisis to resolve or a significant problem to remedy. It's important that you perceive how the overall situation impacts the listener's attentiveness. Is everyone capable of hearing what you have to say, or is the situation so overwhelming that you must first provide consolation before any message will filter through? For most nontrivial concepts to penetrate, the listener must be calm and alert, without overwhelming guilt or remorse. He must not be conflicted, and remain focused, logical, and fluent in the language. Any of these that are out of balance can skew or obliterate the message. I was recently asked to provide advice to an executive faced with a sudden and potentially catastrophic legal challenge. Although the path to a favorable resolution was clear, he didn't hear half of what I had to say, because he couldn't get past the ruinous outcome if his predicament became public by being escalated into a court action. My first task was to calm him down, then convince him that logic didn't support a doom-and-gloom approach. I presented strategic alternatives, and finally personally arranged for legal support to resolve the issue. Had I merely related a set of instructions, and not recognized that his distress was incapacitating, I wouldn't have been much help. We've all been there, and should reflect upon what it means to be confused or distraught.

"Mr. Holton, I'm afraid I've got bad news for you. The magnetic resonance imaging shows that you have a mass near the infero-lateral border of the right ureteropelvic junction. Your creatine phosphokinase is elevated and suggests an inborn error of metabolism consistent with uric acid overproduction, which might be amenable to administration of a xanthine oxidase inhibitor." Whoa! Bad news? How bad is "bad"? A mass? Does that mean I have cancer? What border was that? What the hell is an "inborn error of metabolism"? Xanthine oxidase? This is worse than Greek, it's frightening English, and it sounds like something is very wrong with me.

Let's try this, instead. "Mr. Holton, one of your tests, the MRI scan where you went into the machine for a half hour yesterday, has given us some useful information. It looks like you probably have a kidney stone lodged at the point where the tube from your right kidney empties into your bladder. Based on your lab tests, it seems you may suffer from mild gout, which means that the stone would likely be composed of uric acid. The good news is that there are some medicines that can be expected to control this situation, even though you may have already lost a small amount of kidney function. This isn't uncommon, and certainly not a cause for panic." Still lots of questions, but this time it's obvious that nobody is going to die in the next two hours.

In the midst of the hustle and bustle, or in a calm moment in the presence of a quiet person whose linguistic capabilities you don't know, it's easy to assume that everybody understands everybody. However, this is often not the case. The most commonly neglected element of communication is to ask at appropriate intervals whether you are being understood, particularly when explaining a difficult concept or using a lot of jargon and acronyms. The same holds true if you are the listener. I find it much better to admit my ignorance early on and demand explanations of unfamiliar concepts than to get to the end of a discussion and have to track all the way back to the beginning.

Use plain English (or whatever language you speak). Short discussions are nice, and much less likely to become confusing. If you really want people to understand your logic trail, make your points at the beginning of the conversation, provide commentary in the middle, and then make your points again at the end.

Mind Reading Is Not Effective Communication

Doctors can be lousy communicators for a variety of reasons. First, medical schools have only recently begun to really emphasize teaching the humanitarian component of doctoring. Compared to the amount of science crammed into the medical school curriculum, there's minimal teaching about the psychology of being a doctor. Role playing and interview techniques are generally given short shrift, and little time is devoted to exploring feelings about chronic illness, death and dying, compassion, and patient education techniques. Computer science, cost-effectiveness, and medical record documentation are easier to teach, have quantifiable relevance, and are pressing issues. Second, many medical students are chosen for high test scores and grades, not for the "softer" side of their personalities. Doctors are selected to be achievers in what has traditionally been a pyramidal system of promotion. They are a highly talented and therefore highly competitive group, more often iconoclasts than team players. Third, the confrontations with illness and suffering are plunges, not gradual entries, and many young doctors withdraw, rather than empathize. This is often a necessary, although not desirable, act of self-preservation. Without mentoring, sensitivity to humans is a long-term adjustment achieved over years of patient encounters. Fourth, patients have a love-hate relationship with their doctors, who are held to a higher standard than other professionals in terms of performance and outcomes. Fifth, most physicians possess a knowledge base that can be difficult to translate effectively into lay language, and this situation is made even more difficult because patients hear (and want to hear) different things depending upon their state of health and emotional needs. Finally, the subject matter is profound and deserves extra time for explanation, while the constraints of managed care have forced physicians to delegate their time differently, which translates into less time per patient.

Informed laypersons may know the jargon, but they have the same emotional needs for explanations and reassurance as less sophisticated and more seemingly dependent patients. How information is communicated is a function of respect as well as content. One can never take for granted that the message is fully appreciated and understood. If a patient feels that I am being overexplanatory or talking down to him, I would prefer to be corrected and to adjust my level of discourse than to be misunderstood or incomplete. If I'm unsure of the quality or magnitude of reception, I will often ask a patient to explain back to me, in his own words, what we have discussed. Any hint of a quizzical look or raised eyebrow leads me to attempt a different explanation. I make no assumptions, and never assume that a patient can read my mind. Many times, the critical nature of the situation or the degree of illness has caused the patient's mind to wander, and so we must go back over the same issues again and again.

For corporate executive, the analogy runs true. Theoretically, your top managers have been hired because they possess certain expertise, and therefore can follow your train of thought, even if you jump off at the wrong station. But that's a risky assumption. Why do executives communicate poorly? First, they have a lot of things on their mind, and may seek abbreviated interactions. For fear of seeming ignorant, a manager may not question his boss or seek clarification. Second, in some corporate environments, intrigue is a management technique deployed to hold power over subordinates. This is foolish and nonproductive. Third, many executives have risen from technical positions where they were never taught how to communicate properly. Physician executives, pay attention. Lastly, it's a busy world, and meetings are the bane of corporate existence.

A great team in action is a joy to behold. If you pay close attention, you'll notice that what really sets a team apart is the way that each member is able to anticipate the actions and reactions of the other members. In sports, it's the quarterback-receiver combination; in medicine it's a surgeon and a great scrub nurse. The correct instruments are chosen and slapped into the hand of the operator silently and with unerring accuracy. What allows this phenomenon? Repetition. I promise you that if this were the first time that the doctor had performed this particular surgery, or it was the first time that this assistant ever operated with the doctor, there would need to be a whole lot of talking. Until there is some familiarity with situations and people have had a chance to understand the preferences of their teammates, communication needs to be copious and explicit. An All-Star team is rarely as impressive as the league champion.

I have reasons why I like to apply plaster casts a certain way. I believe that certain structural configurations are stronger and more stable. I don't like rough edges, and I like the artistic challenge of turning a lump of chalk and padding into a semiattractive functional design. When one of my subordinates in the E.R. puts someone in plaster, I expect to see a design that meets with my approval. How would anyone know what I want without an explanation, or having seen an example?

When a situation arises that requires a response, you have a choice of doing the work yourself or delegating it. If you want someone to behave in a certain way, you have to tell them or teach them. You can't expect people to read your mind. Not communicating properly is worsened if you express dissatisfaction at the solution into which you had no input in the first place. This is not to say that you don't have a right to be disappointed or even angry if someone shows substandard abilities or judgment. Rather, I am cautioning you as a manager to be able to differentiate between someone who should have known better and someone who couldn't have known better because you neglected to tell them. You become a micromanager when you usurp the appropriate decision-making authority from those who should be independent thinkers. It can be a tough challenge, particularly in a larger organization, but is probably one of the most frequently flawed behaviors in a senior manager.

If I end up being known for a few things, I hope one of them is that my people never had to read my mind about knowing how I wanted things done. This requires a conscious effort to bring people together and to share opinions, reactions, and expectations.

Paul S. Auerbach, M.D.

Manage against Disabilities to Attain
Maximal Productivity

In many industries, work-related disabilities can be the greatest potential liability for an employer. For persons that work in the E.R., common disabilities are back injuries (specifically, low back strain from lifting and moving patients), slips and falls, being punctured with a needle that's been used on a patient, and emotional fatigue (including "burnout"). In addition, health-care workers suffer their fair share of depression and substance abuse. It's a high-stress environment.

Avoiding disabilities is obviously a more satisfying strategy than treating disabilities. But if you think about it, the rationale goes far beyond lowering absenteeism and workers' compensation claims. It goes to the heart of what's necessary to promote productivity.

Here's how it works. To avoid the disabilities mentioned above, the E.R. needs an education program, regular assessment of the physical and emotional demands placed upon its workers, ergonomic analysis to minimize activities that lead to injuries and to implement methods and rules to maximize assistance at critical times, counseling and incident stress debriefings after particularly emotional events, equipment review to bring the best and safest devices and drug administration paraphernalia into the E.R., and drug control systems to monitor the dispensing and utilization of narcotics and other medications. When you add this all up, what you find is that not only do adverse events diminish, but a much safer and user-friendly work environment has been created. The staff now has a clear view of the impact of the job upon its collective and individual mental health, and persons who are on the edge are identified early, not just after they've cracked. The mandatory education creates a framework for elective education, because the learning process brings the doctors and nurses closer together. Managing against disabilities therefore does all of those functional things that lead to a happier workforce, which soon becomes more productive. Satisfied employees stay longer and, therefore, the average job experience goes up. In the E.R. environment, experience counts for a lot, so the place runs a whole lot smoother with established teams than with high turnover.

In any business, the most common causes of disability should become well known. If you manage to control or eliminate these, you will have a healthier, happier, and more productive staff. The only persons who will resist are the malingerers. In following this advice, you will create a safer environment, amenable to change and allied with the best interests of the workers. It will commonly be their suggestions that lead to improvements. Pay heed to both physical and emotional health, and reward maintenance of a more productive status.

When You Look in the Mirror, What Do You See?

Doctors are justifiably proud. To attain an education and build a practice, a doctor studies for years, makes significant personal and financial sacrifices, and works long hours. To endure the intensities of medical practice and to generate thick skin where political and emotional flames burn hot, it's necessary to develop an ego. With ego comes an external personality. Sometimes your persona reflects your core, and sometimes it's a shell. Intentionally or not, senior managers wear costumes, and are prone to role playing.

What is a stereotypical physician? Complex. Confident, intelligent, empathetic, industrious. Vain, domineering, inflexible, wealthy. We're healers and dictators at the same time. It puts our patients in an awkward position. They want to be cared for, not dominated. When young doctors look up to their mentors, they want to be taught, not browbeaten. There have been times in career as a physician leader when I've been badly out of touch, talking down to patients and harassing my trainees. When it becomes apparent, even to me, I stare into the mirror.

Senior management is about leadership, competence, confidence, and communication. We all strive to maintain a high profile in each of these, but sometimes we fail. When that happens, how do we find out? Are there people comfortable (or uncomfortable) enough to tell us? Are we sufficiently cognizant of our behavior's impact to know when an adjustment is necessary? Where are the mirrors, and who bothers to use them?

You can preen or you can observe. The reflection is helpful only if you keep your eyes open and turn on the light. Self-assessment is painful, but essential if you intend to grow as a person. Unfortunately, most senior managers grow too busy or set in their ways to focus on their own behaviors. Furthermore, we begin to believe that we've somehow earned the right to avoid an assessment. A 360-degree evaluation is ideal, but at a minimum, take the time to get in front of the mirror and just look up and down. Do you like what you see? Be honest. If you're fortunate enough to have children, ask them and they will tell you.

Everybody Wears a Medal

People work for different rewards. Everybody likes to be appreciated, but often in different ways. Have you ever asked your employees what gives them the greatest satisfaction and how they would most like to be rewarded for outstanding performance? Allowing people to work in an environment that provides opportunity for self-fulfillment is essential. But don't assume that a bonus check is the best bonus for everybody.

The first time I attended a banquet of the National Association for Search and Rescue, it seemed that nearly everybody in attendance received an award for one accomplishment or another. The awards were mostly medals, and the recipients were thrilled. What I learned was that although the acts of service and heroism performed by these people were in and of themselves amazing events, the cycle was completed only upon presentation of a piece of metal attached to a ribbon. It wasn't about money or fame—it was about high esteem in the eyes of one's peers.

In the E.R., the professional managers are pragmatic and stoic, because highs and lows don't work well in a potentially volatile environment. For everyone else, the activities that might contribute to job satisfaction are too numerous to mention. Yet it is automatic that patient outcomes are the be-all and end-all of what makes the employees strive to do a good job. Even though the contributions of registration clerks, lab technicians, and x-ray techs are essential to an efficient process, most of the time these persons never learn the ultimate outcome for their patients. So it's difficult to provide the sort of emotional rewards that might be achieved by a nurse or doctor.

Feedback can come in many forms, but for the sake of simplicity, I consider it to be immediate or delayed, and public or private. That gives four combinations, and I try to use them all. When a resident neatly repairs a wound, I take her aside and offer praise, which coming from me is a big deal. When an aide puts up the side rails on a gurney so that the patient can't roll off and fall to the floor, I thank him loudly, so that everyone can see that what he did was important and appreciated. When I receive a letter from a patient who mentions the sympathetic approach taken by a registration clerk, I thank the clerk in private and inform him that I am placing this letter of praise in his personnel file. When someone of good nature has worked in the department for a decade, she becomes the recipient of a gift at a social gathering of the employees.

Money is appreciated, but should always be accompanied by something that can be displayed proudly. The award should be a message to the employee and to everyone else that these achievements are genuinely appreciated, and that they are important. Find every possible way that you can honor those that seek to be excellent. There shouldn't be an employee in your company who isn't eligible for some kind of award.

Don't Get Excited Unless You're Happy

The reference here is to expressions of emotion that are frightening to a patient who hangs on the doctor's every word. A doctor should never say "Whoops!," "That's the most disgusting thing I've ever seen," or "This is a hopeless situation." Frustration, anger, fear, and despair are the human emotions that require the greatest skill and depth of relationships to articulate without creating a negative effect. A patient is constantly looking for affirmation that the situation is under control and that the doctor both understands what's happening and what's likely to happen. Any indication that the patient is not being taken seriously, is in jeopardy, or may be failing generates sinking emotions that can seriously damage the doctor-patient relationship or patient's ability to deal effectively with his predicament.

Paul S. Auerbach, M.D.

On the other hand, enthusiasm for care and an expression of interest in the particulars of a specific patient's condition or disease can be hugely supportive. A patient can tell when you are being genuine and want to share his sense of accomplishment and relief in the healing process. He wants to be contributory, and can do this better if the doctor lets him into his thought process, allowing the patient to participate. In doing so, the physician must be careful to reveal the details, but not to raise unnecessary or unfounded preliminary concerns that could be upsetting.

Mood swings are a no-no. If it's one thing that drives people crazy, it's having to react to a leader who wears his heart on his sleeve. Running a clinic or a business is not like performing in an opera. Ultimately, the manic operator forces his underlings or charges to turn him off, because to do otherwise is to be subjected to an emotional roller coaster.

It's easy to form early impressions, but a doctor needs to keep them to himself until there's enough evidence to formulate reasoned opinions. This is both prudent from a litigation perspective and also when one considers that shooting from the hip often generates erroneous statements and leaves a bad impression that the shooter is poorly informed and judgmental. Remember, the truth always lies somewhere in the middle. Dealing from strength as a manager means above all else dealing from a position of experience reinforced with timely and accurate information.

While there are certainly successful examples of senior managers who can be ebullient and effective, this is a much riskier path than keeping an even keel and appearing in tighter control of one's emotions. There's room for variation, but one thing is certain—outbursts of negativity are demoralizing, particularly if they occur in public. Discipline, which is necessary, should occur behind closed doors.

If you're an emotive person, this can be a difficult recommendation. Many people have styles that have them wrapped up in the moment. A theatrical presentation can be very entertaining. However, it can be quite disturbing to the uninitiated and is more commonly misinterpreted than an even-keeled delivery. I'm not advocating unfriendliness, or trying to suppress a deserved moment of joy or levity. Rather, I hearken back to the notion that a person in a senior management position is guiding a family that keys into his every word, every smile, and every frown. Without becoming paternalistic or maternalistic, become a positive mentor and a role model, then act accordingly.

Act professionally at all times, including the Christmas party. Don't be trapped by an informal atmosphere in which you may be lulled into a false sense of security. The reference here is not only to emotional outbursts and expressions of emotion, but to subtle inuendoes that are always subject to misinterpretation. In a medical setting, fatigue and frustration stoke ill-advised comments; at a social event, too many drinks make you stupid.

Paul S. Auerbach, M.D.

Burning Bridges Leads to Long Falls

That having been said, it doesn't mean that you can't throw somebody off a bridge from time to time. The preferred approach is to cut with precision, not to lop off an entire limb to cure a wart.

Nothing is more tempting than to take a broad-brush approach to a particular problem and to attempt to generalize a solution, because a more targeted approach would be arduous or inconvenient. This goes double when you're under attack or feeling argumentative.

A teenage quarterback came to the E.R. He might have been knocked unconscious for a few seconds (no one really knew), but was completely awake when the paramedics lifted him onto a stretcher to be hauled off the field. In the ambulance on the way to the hospital, the young man vomited once. By the time he was examined by me, he was awake, alert, and oriented to who he was, where he was, and why he was there. He said he had a headache, but wanted to go home. His neck didn't hurt and I couldn't even find a bump on his head. His neurological exam was normal, so my initial decision was to watch him for a while, to avoid the expense of a computed tomographic (CT) brain scan. After I explained my reasoning to his mother, she was comfortable with my decision.

Unfortunately, his coach wasn't. As it turned out, the injured football player had a big game coming up and his coach wanted him to be able to practice as soon as possible. When I told him that not obtaining a brain scan would make me recommend at least a four-day interval before resuming contact sports, the coach argued strongly for an immediate determination of the extent of the injury, which could only be accomplished with a brain scan. He named one of the neurosurgeons on staff, with whom I had never had direct contact, and demanded that he be contacted immediately. I made the communication.

What I didn't know was that this particular neurosurgeon didn't trust E.R. doctors, had been in the operating room all day, and was in a bad mood. He stormed into the patient's cubicle, performed a quick exam, and then proceeded to shout at me and anyone else who cared to listen.

"Goddammit! What are you bothering me for? This boy doesn't need a scan. Whose idea was it to call me down here?"

"The boy's coach. He said you were a family friend."

"He's full of it. What's your name again?"

"Auerbach. I'm the Chief of Emergency Medicine." By this time, everyone within earshot was listening, including the boy's mother. I wasn't worried about her son's health, just how to do public relations damage control.

"Well, I don't give a rat's ass if you're the Pope. Do whatever you want. Get a scan or don't get a scan, I don't care. Now I'm leaving. Got any other life and death situations you need me to resolve for you?" My entire staff was now watching to see how I was going to manage this misanthrope.

What were my choices? My first instinct was to pull rank and chew the man out in front of the staff, patient, and patient's family. However, if I stooped to his level, then I automatically would be at fault because no matter what happens, no one has the right to misbehave in a patient care area. That makes you wrong, even when you're right. I decided to discipline the miscreant, but not destroy a potentially more important relationship. I led him into my office and asked him to apologize to the patient for his rude behavior. He declined the opportunity and gave me another tongue-lashing.

The next morning, I visited with the Chief of Neurosurgery and informed him what had happened. Then I told him that I would no longer accept this particular physician as a consultant in the E.R., which would severely impact the call schedule. The Neurosurgery Chief said he understood and that it wouldn't happen again. The offender called me to apologize. The bridge was left intact.

This was the business of medicine used to reinforce appropriate interpersonal behavior. No business operation of any size gets through a day without the identification of a problem, adverse event, or interpersonal conflict. The sloppy reactive manager shouts, sweeps with a big broom, or even makes threats. The precise manager will take the brief moments necessary to gather all the facts, aim the response carefully, and take care to push only those who deserved to be pushed.

Who Cares How They Do Things at UCLA?

I did my residency in Emergency Medicine at UCLA. My first job out of training was as a faculty physician in the E.R. at Temple University Hospital in Philadelphia. It was a busy inner-city E.R. that saw lots of trauma and served as the safety net for a large indigent population with no other access to health care. The nurses and technicians who worked in the E.R. were seasoned veterans with a whole lot more practical experience than me. Sometimes their way of doing things was idiosyncratic, but it worked well in that environment.

I thought I was hot stuff. Every other word out of my mouth was, "This is how we did it at UCLA." Some of my suggestions were OK, but none was earth-shaking. Furthermore, I never found an occasion to comment anything to the effect that I liked the way they did things at Temple or that I was learning anything new. I *was* learning, but didn't recognize *the need to point out what was right as well as what was wrong.* I was irritating everyone.

One afternoon, after I rearranged all the tubes hanging on the wall in the cardiac room, commenting that this was how they were arranged at UCLA, one of the nurses pulled me aside. "Paul," she whispered, "If you tell anybody one more time how they do things at UCLA, I'm gonna rip your *%#$@& tongue out. Nobody cares how they do things at UCLA. You're at Temple now."

Her words were a bucket of cold water. I felt like an idiot, but realized that she chastised me out of concern.

I moved the tubes back. It was a lesson I've never forgotten.

When you enter into a new situation, particularly when you have the authority to make changes, you have to respect people for what they know and seek to understand why things are the way they are. Your "better way to do things" may indeed one day prove to be better, but if you feel the need to change everything right away and all at once, understand that you will offend people. Their established ways involve more than old habits. For many, these represent stability and a way of life, pathways they use to guide them through complex and difficult situations. Show some respect for the local expertise, even if you find that you eventually need to make changes.

Don't Become Obsessed with Popularity

Popularity is nice, but don't forget that what drives genuine respect and affection for a manager may sometimes involve unpopular managerial practices. There are things you have to do for patients that are painful in the short run, but intended to be beneficial in the long run. A doctor can do less or do it differently and make a patient happy, but that may not be the best thing. I can walk through the E.R. and keep my mouth shut or point out what needs to be corrected: bedrails that need to be raised, patients who should be covered with warm blankets, I.V.s that need to be restarted, too much loud chatter in the hallways. Pushing people to perform to my expectations does not win popularity contests, but it is absolutely the responsibility of a diligent manager. This generates compliance, so what counts is how to do it in such a way as to create partners in the practice. If you get to the point where you want to elicit affection, then do some of the dirty work yourself and don't be a blatant delegator. Empty a few bedpans. Don't think of yourself as royalty.

As Director of an E.R. or a business, it's impossible to be everyone's friend. There are two main reasons for this. The first is that there are always issues and problems that involve some of your closest employees. When you have to make the hard decisions, it's natural for those nearest to you to anticipate favoritism. But you just can't play favorites. Second, appearing to be too familiar with selected individuals or to single them out for inadvertent affection upsets the natural balance of your leadership. Consistency has to be preserved at all costs.

If you try to drive decisions based upon what you perceive will be popular, or because you believe it will make *you* popular, you run the risk of being labeled a politician for the wrong reasons. Being a lead physician in an E.R. doesn't provide many strokes if you expect constant reassurance of your value as a leader who can make all the employees happy. Your major responsibility is to take care of patients, and to see that others take care of them just as well.

Your popularity is at greatest risk when you are implementing a reorganization, because you are eliminating jobs, shifting people out of their comfort zones, and effecting change, all of which contribute to anxiety. People don't like to be anxious, which translates into negative energy. Given the propensity for most folks to look for a scapegoat, your popularity will wane. Don't fall into the trap of managing to quell the resistance. Stand your ground and provide continuous information while taking meaningful feedback. But don't lose your momentum for the sake of a pat on the back or a more heartfelt smile. It's important to take people through a few tough times to see how well they will stick with you when they aren't particularly enamored of what you're trying to accomplish.

TOOLS OF THE TRADE

It's virtually impossible for a medical practitioner to keep up with scientific advances and commit them to useful memory. The real value of information technology and the Internet in medicine will be to enable instant differential diagnosis and therapeutic decisions based upon the latest information. Automation and instrumentation are gradually replacing eyes and ears. One can only hope that the therapeutic touch will not become robotic. I see the same advances in the corporate suite, as leaders now respond to integrated triggers set off by acute data acquisition not possible even a few years ago. You don't need my help with that. However, leaders are defined by their intellect, fortitude, ethics, ego, endurance, and disposition. You make decisions that require more skill than spread sheet analysis. It's not enough to know the right things to do—you must actually do them. In this section, take some of the methods I've used in the E.R. and let them work for you.

Recognize When You Are Being Tested

The E.R. is a tough place, a true fishbowl in the parlor of medicine. I remember one day after I had just become the E.R. Director at a major medical center. I participated in the care of a patient of a famous transplant surgeon. The ill woman had come to the E.R. complaining of weakness, difficulty breathing, and abdominal pain. She had undergone a heart-lung transplant a few months previously, and this was her first presentation with symptoms of organ rejection. Her medication list was a mile long. To be honest, the resident and I didn't recognize many of the drugs, which were beyond our area of expertise. At least one medication was experimental. Part of the patient's problem was asthma, so the resident ordered some tests and began treatment, to which the patient responded favorably. I put in a call to the surgeon to inform him that his patient was in the E.R.

Fifteen minutes later this surgeon pillar grabbed my arm in the hallway, put his nose up to my face, and said, "Can't you guys get *anything* right? *Everyone* knows my patients are supposed to go on steroids. Who the hell are you? What the hell are you doing? I want to be called for *everything* from now on."

From a medical perspective, on a scale of one to ten, this was a zero. The patient was doing great, and the therapy chosen by the resident was just fine. Furthermore, I knew that this particular professor had a reputation for testing new people. There was even a twinkle in his eye as he sought to intimidate me. I looked behind me and saw a few people peeking around the corner. The resident was petrified, but I'd been there before.

In a friendly tone, I addressed the surgeon by his first name and said, "You know, you could be up in the operating room doing a transplant, and you could take an ice pick and stick it into somebody's heart, and *nobody* would ever find out about it. But down here in the E.R., we put a Band-Aid on crooked, and everybody in the hospital hears about it. You know, this isn't such a big deal. By the way, it's nice to meet you. I'm the new Director of the E.R. I've been a fan of yours for years."

We shook hands, he turned and gave the resident an icy look, just to keep up appearances, then walked out the door. From that point forward, he was always one of the E.R.'s strongest advocates.

Well, what if I hadn't reacted the way I did? What if I had tried to go one-on-one with this icon? We would have brawled, metaphorically speaking, and I would have come out the loser. One of us had to step back for a moment and recognize the encounter for what it was. I was being tested, to see if I was deferential to authority, had a backbone, owned a sense of humor, and was interested more in getting along or in getting my way. This encounter was illustrative of the fact that most administrative tests come when it may appear that nothing is at stake. That is, this patient was just fine and everybody knew it. The episode was just an excuse to test the new kid on the block.

I was the recipient of a different test on another day, this time in the COO chair, with the challenge coming from the opposite direction on the organization chart. It came in the form of indignation, a complaint that someone hadn't been well informed on an issue that really didn't have anything to do with him. Why wasn't his name on the distribution list, when he was so *important*? How was he supposed to *manage* (he wasn't a manager) when he wasn't kept in the loop, like the other managers?

My initial reaction was to be apologetic. But after a little reflection, I became annoyed. This was a person with an attitude, not someone who was trying to get brought up to speed. My response was to do what I absolutely hate, but that comes with the territory. I applied discipline. I reminded the complainer that his style of communication was inappropriately confrontational and his approach didn't match up with my understanding of his position in the organization or with his accomplishments. In short, he needed to prove himself to me, not vice versa.

Still, I realized that this expression of dissatisfaction needed to be mined for the kernel of distress, even if the

Paul S. Auerbach, M.D.

messenger or method was unpleasant. The man who complained hadn't been communicated with very well, which was someone else's fault. Applying a remedy to that situation proved beneficial to the organization as a whole, although I am certain that this isn't what my complainer had in mind.

Who is allowed to administer a test? Just about anyone, but that carries certain risk. Is the test educational or is it designed to intimidate? Is your intent to challenge someone, and if so, is your timing correct? Are you flexing your ego or are you trying to accomplish something useful? Think about your personal reactions when you are tested. Whenever my family complains that I'm spending too much time at work and not enough time with them, it's really a test. Does he still care about us? Does he love us? The complaints have a purpose. If I move in the wrong direction, it won't have the intended effect, that's for sure. My first reaction, if I'm tired, is to resent the question. Don't they understand? Can't they appreciate that I'm doing this all for them? Then, when I get some rest or a few hours of sleep, I realize that the test is really another chance to get it right. They want me to pass. On the other hand, I have a tougher time with "needy" people at work. These folks are supposed to be professional, to carry their own weight, to leave their neurotic baggage behind. But that's not the way it works, if you understand anything at all about people. In a senior management position, you have to be the grand strategist and, at the same time, you have to continuously help people adjust their personal needs in relation to the business requirements of the organization. In an executive role, you are constantly being tested for consistency and favor. The number of communications that are straightforward and that can be taken at face value are outweighed ten to one by those which must be dissected for the true message, which is often the simple two-part question, "Where are you? Where am I?"

A Terminal Situation
Benefits from a Team Approach

An ending is difficult, whether it represents a dying patient or a failing business. In the former, the anguish is obvious, even though death may represent relief from suffering. In the latter, termination of a business unit, dissolution of a grand strategy that failed, or the natural attrition of a concept whose time has passed is understandably somber and disappointing.

The burden of guiding a person to the end of his life is a defining moment in medicine, which sets a physician apart from other professionals. It isn't for everyone. A cancer specialist faces death and dying with regularity, so must develop an empathetic approach and sensitivity that don't become self-destructive. Viewed for the opportunity to assist a patient in his greatest time of need, the burden is transformed into an opportunity.

Demise and death often progress in stages, such that an organized response is possible. There are many issues,

Paul S. Auerbach, M.D.

such as patient comfort, family finances, grief support, asset distribution, child custody, and funeral arrangements. It's unrealistic to expect any physician to be expert in all these matters. In recognition, a cohesive approach has arisen. This is the care team, so that experts can meet regularly and participate in care planning, to assist the patient and physician in resolving all the issues and tasks attendant to death. This is a marvelous development, as it enables multiple points of contact and viewpoints to maintain focus upon the most important element—supporting the patient and family. In addition, a team allows its members to identify the impact of a patient's death upon the caregivers. In an E.R. after a particularly disturbing episode, such as the sudden death of a small child, debriefing among team members is critically important.

In a business, a program may fail for many reasons. The structure or concept may have been ill-conceived, the program undercapitalized, the competition too dominant, or the personnel ineffective. One is always tempted to "pull the plug" when there is financial hemorrhage. Sometimes, this is absolutely necessary and there isn't any time for the niceties. However, more often the terminal disease has been diagnosed for quite some time, and there's an opportunity to put together a care team to assist in the dying. There are issues: reallocation of resources, public notification, personnel placement and outsourcing, and the disappointment associated with what is invariably viewed as failure. Senior managers should guide team members by stating clearly the reasons for the business termination and the lessons to be learned. As opposed to a natural human death, which sets its own schedule, a business unit death may occur according to a schedule. The team can allow the stages of death and dying to be orderly, and avoid the shock of sudden grief at an unanticipated loss. Learning from failure is often cited as a goal, but this is very difficult when fingers are being pointed and everyone is trying to save his own skin. The senior manager is in the best position to set a tone of reconciliation and healing, rather than blame. As death is an inevitable consequence of birth, so too is the demise or transformation of a company the inevitable consequence of its creation. Companies that are willing to adapt and change may live longer, but no company lasts forever.

We All Live in Glass Houses

There is a certain type of error that is only made by the politically inept resident-in-training at the academic hospital. Small community hospitals, particularly in a rural environment, do not have the resources of large university trauma centers. Out in the sticks, a single doctor and nurse may staff the E.R. There's no backup for this team. No neurosurgeon, no chest surgeon, no MRI scanner, no angiography suite—nothing but basic equipment and the two hands that God gave them. In rolls a motorcycle accident victim with both legs shattered, blood in his chest, and massive facial injuries. It's all the doctor and

153

nurse can do to keep the patient alive, let alone perform a perfect resuscitation. They apply all manner of splints and bandages, call for a helicopter, and evacuate the patient to "the Mecca." When the patient arrives at the big center, he only has one I.V., because that's all his doctor could do. One of the splints has loosened and there's a big cut left uncovered by a bandage. The package could have been neater, but the victim got to the right facility quickly, which is incredibly important.

As the patient is wheeled down the hall from the heliport and into our E.R., his wife rushes in from the waiting room in time to listen to the surgery intern announce to no one in particular, "Man, who took care of this patient? He should have had three big lines. Look at this splint. What a joke. And look at all this blood. Why did they leave this open? What a mess."

What a stupid, insensitive thing to say. This young buck doesn't have any idea what it's like to practice without support, or the visceral fear of a doctor faced with a badly crunched victim and lacking the resources to handle the situation in an ideal fashion. What Big Mouth should have done was step back and admire the incredible job performed under adverse circumstances, and praised the performance. If he couldn't do that, he should have just kept his tirade to himself.

It's easy to be critical, especially when you weren't there. I think the older we get as managers, the more tolerant we become (or should become) for the obstacles faced by everyday operations, particularly in situations of limited resources. A trainee has no grounds to sit in an ivory tower and preen about the deficiencies of those who are unlike him. Let him become skillful first, and then let him demonstrate his wisdom by teaching. When you manage, select for the maturity that belies the measure of years. Challenge those who would interact by challenging others, and determine whether they are fair competitors; if they aren't, put them in their place by keeping them away from your precious customers.

Inbreeding Doesn't Advance the Genome

Medical centers have a way of holding onto their own. We tend to be comfortable surrounding ourselves with people we know, for many good reasons. We can vouch for their level of training and knowledge base, have observed their performance in critical situations, and have grown to like them as individuals. There is guaranteed compatibility. The same is true in any business.

However, there's a risk to not going outside for new people. A corporate culture can quickly become a barrier to entry for new ideas, as employees become reticent to take chances in front of their friends. If the business stalls for any period of time, there may be no growth, and important new concepts need to be generated internally. If you have a strongly creative environment this might work, but I can think of hardly any situation where there is not enormous benefit from a different perspective, if only to validate the truths we hold so dear.

If you find yourself in a holding pattern, then create a contest for new initiatives or start sending your people outside to attend conferences, take classes, and see what's going on. Evolution depends on diversification, and is thwarted by inbreeding.

In the venture capital business, there's another reason to diversify. Retaining technical proficiency is very difficult when you switch from being a scientist or executive to being an investor. Biotechnology is an excellent example. The breadth of the advances and the depth at which they must be understood preclude a person of normal intellect from staying sufficiently current to make perfect decisions. The best way to broaden your reach is to bring in a person with the *recent* expertise and connections to get good advice quickly when you need it. If you seek a person who is so much like you that you can be confused for siblings, you are reinforcing your quirks, not expanding your horizons.

The First Time a Person Quits, Let Him Go

A harsh admonition like this may seem counter to the thematic spirit of this book, but it reflects the reality of how things in all likelihood will go after a person first offers to resign. This is particularly true if someone plays the resignation card in anger, either because he can't get his way or as an act of extortion. You can try to coerce a person to stay, but you're better off letting an unhappy person go and directing your energies toward the people willing to fight the good fight.

The patient who is ill and tired, perhaps undergoing chemotherapy or a series of painful surgeries, may want to quit, which is understandable. In this circumstance, it's the physician's duty to be sympathetic, to offer reasonable assurances of what the future might hold depending upon what decisions are made, and to counsel the patient in a reasonable course of action. Ultimately, it's the patient's choice, but enormous weight is given to the doctor's opinion, because the substance and theories of medicine are so removed from the layperson's framework of understanding. The employee who has struggled with a business project or sales assignment, and who is failing, may also wish to throw in the towel. Managers tend to be far less sympathetic because they focus on the inadequacies, often under the assumption that a person has been hired to do a job, and is supposed to get it done. This may be a reasonable approach, but it may ignore the potential to rectify the situation. You have to make an assessment of how a person has qualified himself for a task, measure the personal representations and warranties, tally the performance, and decide if there has been a failure that requires discipline or a penalty, or whether the system has failed the participant.

When a patient "fires" a doctor, it's often because of failed communication or extreme disappointment. The relationship is declining, and there's a lack of confidence or diminished trust. When a doctor refuses to care for a patient, which is a rare event, the patient has either ignored the doctor's advice, refused to meet a financial obligation, or shown significant disrespect to the doctor, which can include a gratuitous threat of litigation. If mutual respect is necessary to consummate a transaction and if that trust cannot be attained, then it's best to sever rather than to suffer.

When an employee comes to me and says "give me a raise or I'll leave," I do a quick analysis to see if the compensation request is reasonable. If it is, but the employee never came in first to ask for a raise without the ultimatum, I'm inclined to let him go unless there's no way I can live without him. Some people will quit just to get you to beg them to stay. That's a weak way for a person to behave and doesn't speak well for the future. So I say, "Good luck and let me know if I can provide a reference."

With a doctor who wants to leave medicine, it's tougher. There are so many reasons to become discouraged. Dealing with death and dying, long hours, separation from family, the depersonalization inherent in medical training, and many other stressors can lead a doctor to want to quit. This is an opportunity to counsel for a change of venue or to send someone on a vacation. However, if the well-rested dermatologist wants to quit, let him go, because it isn't going to get any better.

Don't Run a Special on Appendicitis, unless You Have Fifty Surgeons Ready to Operate

The E.R. is the recipient of real disease and perceived disease. Anyone who has worked there long enough has cared for periodic waves of patients whose visits were generated by the media. Whenever there's a television or radio program that features appendicitis, Lyme disease, or heart attacks, the E.R. gets swamped with people who imagine that they're suffering. People are very "suggestible," particularly when it comes to their health. The most provocative conclusion to any of these media programs is, "If you have any of these problems, immediately seek medical attention." While that statement may not be valid from a public health perspective, it's always necessary as a disclaimer so that the producer of the program doesn't get sued. Besides, who can practice medicine over the phone? An examination is worth a thousand words.

There, I just did it. It happens that easily. I suggested to you what ailment you might have, or should have, and then said the only way to find out is to come in so I can examine you. You can pretend it's a lot of things, but what actually just happened is the anatomy of a sale. So, your marketing people go out and tell everybody about your new service, except it's not a service you actually have. It's one you might be ready to offer in six weeks. This typifies the classic conflict between marketing and operations. Your salespeople eat raw meat and have an incentive to sell, while the operations people have to deliver on what's been sold. If there's a single meeting that needs to occur with regularity in any company where sales and marketing are separated from operations, it's a gathering to review the leads, likelihood of closure, and timing of the implementation. No one likes to be sold anything that can't be delivered on time as advertised. I only let my vendors make that mistake one time, and then only with a good excuse, before I don't give them the opportunity to burn me again.

For Pete's Sake, Read the Documents *before* You Go into the Meeting

Doctors blow this one all the time. In the E.R., it's amazing how many times we leap into therapy prior to reviewing the patient's medical record. That makes sense when you're faced with a cardiac arrest or severe allergic reaction for which the old record isn't necessarily relevant. However, it's potentially wasteful to order a bunch of tests or make noncritical interventions when a brief review of the record would indicate that this is redundant. Why don't we wait for the charts? That's precisely the reason—the magnitude of the wait. Given the lack of electronic integration of records and the need to keep patients moving through the E.R., it is simply an issue of efficiency. However, we pay a price for that, which ultimately gets translated into extra dollars spent and rampant overutilization. My recommendation is that when you have the time, read the chart.

So, having developed a bad habit, the physician executive carries it into the next venue, the corporate suite. Let's say, for example, that in today's meeting a business plan for a new manufacturing unit is going to be reviewed. Used to thinking on my feet, I carry the voluminous supporting documents in my briefcase, unread. I intend to scan them during the meeting if necessary. Of course it will be necessary! So, when we bog down in the details of the financials at the meeting, out come the papers, and I have to try to interpret complicated calculations while listening to a presentation on the marketing approach. I don't do justice to either task, and thereby waste everyone's time.

If the issue revolves around contracts, plans, analyses, or any other written documents, then read them before you go into the meeting. More than that, highlight or isolate the important parts, and write down the issues you wish to have addressed. Understand the history of a situation, and do your homework. If you aren't prepared, then consider postponing the meeting.

The other reason why it's important for you to be prepared is related to positioning. *Someone in the room is going to have done the homework, and it's never strategic to be less well prepared than others, particularly if any aspect of the meeting will relate to negotiation or allocation of resources.* A truly great batter may be able to adapt quickly to a new pitcher, but most will agree that they see the advantage of a few warm-up swings in the on-deck circle.

Paul S. Auerbach, M.D.

Put Your Old Books in a Yard Sale

Medical school and postgraduate training transfer a tremendous amount of knowledge to the students and young doctors, but current curricula are not adequate to support a physician throughout a lengthy career. Certain humanistic themes are timeless, but technical information changes constantly. Every day, there are new tests and therapies discovered, and epidemiological data coalescing to change recommendations for the delivery of care. Therefore, in order to be effective, a physician must commit to a process of continuing education, which is often difficult to maintain because of limited time and access. Many physicians are out of date, which is worsened by the fact that we are all creatures of habit. Doctors tend to fall back on approaches that were ingrained during medical school.

One nice trick to stay current is to put your medical textbooks in a yard sale at least once every five years. Now you need a new reference set. The doctor needs either to go out and acquire a repeat education, buy new books and read them, or bring in younger associates who can teach and treat. Patients deserve no less than current therapies.

This is a common phenomenon with other professionals in scientific or technical fields. As knowledge expands, so must the capabilities of the providers. Often, the solution is to take the technically proficient, but aging, operator and move him into a management role.

That is a good transition when it works, because it lends credibility to the manager, who ought to be attuned to the needs of his employees. Organizations must be proactive and continually reassess how well trained their managers must be. This applies to communications literacy, customer service, data collection, and understanding customers and the market. Like the doctor, however, the senior executive needs to know the field, because his customers are not well served by an ignorant benefactor.

Just Because You Have Money Doesn't Mean You Have to Spend It

Hospitals and physicians are under constant scrutiny because the era preceding managed care was characterized by huge government subsidies for poorly audited programs. Payment for health care was on a cost-plus basis, where the more you billed, the more you made. Spending was profligate. Every patient wanted the newest and the best facilities, equipment, and amenities. Money was not preferentially invested in research and development, but used to lavish attention on the people and agencies that could deliver market share to hospitals.

That type of overconsumption led to an overdue realization that we were going to rapidly exhaust financial resources, without any clear, demonstrable proof that our system was superior to other, less costly, national delivery systems. So now, employers burdened with runaway health care expenditures demand significant reform, faster than can be accomplished by the nemertine legislative process. What was a classic case of certain elements of the medical establishment milking the system to achieve short-term goals (income) without considering the long-term effect (bankruptcy of existing financial resources) upon the delivery system as a whole, led us to market and government interventions. As a result, doctors now and likely forever will have their activities tightly regulated, work longer hours at lower compensation, become more corporate in their behaviors, and consider themselves more employees than entrepreneurs.

The same holds true for companies that choose to spend in order to achieve growth, but not necessarily to create value. Perhaps not by coincidence, this was the phenomenon in the physician practice management company (PPMC) sector. This house of cards aggregated physician practices, purporting to achieve economies of scale by consolidating management services. The perpetrators applied Wall Street multiples to earnings, and then rewarded shareholders handsomely for their investment. However, the compelling part of the story was growth rather than the product. Money was preferentially directed at acquisitions, rather than at achieving true efficiencies, modifying physician behavior, or other forms of true improvement. Furthermore, savings were ignored. Money was lavished on doctors to buy them out of practices, yet no incentives were created to maintain the real business. Look what happened. A lot of share-holder money was lost on this fiasco. Next we had the Internet, then genomics. Guess what's going to happen?

To sell a business, whether in the public marketplace or in a merger situation, I suppose you don't have to really have a business, but it helps. Which is inherently more stable—a house with a foundation that was built off a plan, or an improvised structure thrown together with parts designed for ten different houses?

If you're an architect, then find a good builder. They're not the same. When you assume responsibility for creating sustainable value, it's important to have reserves, for your personal well-being, for your patient's health, for your employee's job satisfaction, and for the future of your company. Seek to support accumulation of the following, so that they can be deployed as needed. These are not rewards—they are essential elements without which components and structures will fail.

- For yourself—rest, sleep, hydration, nutrition, warmth, shelter, the will to live, compassion, and confidence

- For your patients—comfort, self-esteem, autonomy, and hope

- For your employees—loyalty, inquisitiveness, independence, opportunity, diversions, and understanding

- For your company—teamwork, focus, leadership, and capital

Paul S. Auerbach, M.D.

Teach People to Help You

I was jogging up a hilly road on a wintry day when I saw
two dogs looming in the distance. I made a left turn to
avoid them, and stepped on a piece of black ice. My right
foot turned underneath me as I fell onto it with all of my
weight. I heard a distinct "crack" as a flash of intense
pain shot through my ankle. I knew immediately that I
had broken my ankle.

None of my medical school training prepared me for
what followed. As I lay on the road, I held my leg
straight up in the air and grunted in pain, which lasted
for two minutes. The pain was followed by complete
numbness at the site of the injury, as my body responded
with a surge of endorphins. I tried to stand, and heard
my bones crunch as my body moved left and my foot
moved right. I lay back down on the road and inched
myself backwards, dragging my legs behind me, until I
was able to flag down a passing car. The driver and his
wife loaded me into their minivan and delivered me
back to our cabin in the Sierras. My fourteen-year-old
son didn't like what he saw, but he had attended many
wilderness medicine educational programs with me,
where doctors were taught to manage orthopedic
injuries in the field. He fashioned a splint from a card-
board box and applied it to my wobbly foot with adhe-
sive tape. That night I underwent an operation at the
hands of a superb orthopedic surgeon to restore the
anatomy of my ankle.

166

The episode was no fun, but it could have been a lot worse if someone didn't know what to do, or even worse, had panicked. After the initial pain cleared out my head, I knew to stay flat and keep my ankle as motionless as possible. I have the National Ski Patrol Wilderness Emergency Care curriculum to thank for that. The good Samaritans who rescued me from the road knew to cushion me in their vehicle, and how to transfer me into the house, skills likely acquired from a first aid course. My son's Boy Scout training and rapt attention at medical meetings gave him the confidence to take care of his dad. The surgeon who operated on me was prompt, professional, and courteous, because he had treated thousands of patients in his career.

Now it is clear why I have devoted so much of my career teaching emergency and wilderness medicine to doctors and laypeople. It's so they can help me when I get banged up. That's not a bad reason, really.

We all need help from time to time. The scene of a critical incident is not the best place to introduce new rescue concepts. It's a time for rapid response and maximal competence. Senior managers tend to carry the weight of the world on their shoulders, and to restrict empowerment to a precious few individuals. That may be a misguided approach, particularly if you have a distributed organization in which communication is not instantaneous. Face it, you are going to have moments of weakness, confusion, and ineptitude. You will either request assistance or have it proffered by your Board of Directors. In many of these circumstances, a loyal and empowered workforce can avert problems or manage them swiftly for you with a minimum of commotion. The level of education and responsibility should be commensurate with the situations that your allies might encounter. The first step in a medical episode is to attend to life- or limb-threatening problems, then to try to hone in on a diagnosis, to allow less urgent interventions. It's absolutely the same in your business. The total win-win situation is when you provide people with knowledge that can help them be good at what they do, support your business, and pull someone else's fanny out of the fire, should that become necessary.

Technology Is No Substitute for a Cold Cloth on the Forehead

A decade ago, I rafted down the Colorado River in the Grand Canyon as an instructor on a wilderness medicine continuing medical education program. I was one of two physician educators, and the audience was composed of doctors and nurses. The topic was wilderness medicine; that is, how to take care of emergencies when isolated in a rugged environment far from medical assistance. The lectures were designed to be both educational and entertaining. The students were there to learn, but they were also there for fun and adventure.

The other instructor on the trip was young and took his work seriously. He expected the participants to be as well prepared and rigorous in their course work as if they were sitting in a lecture hall at the university. In one session, he used makeup to create a simulated victim, and then asked observers how they might provide medical rescue for some fairly horrible injuries. When one of the students answered incorrectly, he berated him, to the chagrin and, soon, anger, of the student's companion, who felt that the instructor's critical approach was harsh and out of place in this vacation setting.

A day later, the instructor decided he would once again test his students. He confided in me that he was going to pretend to choke while eating lunch and that I should not intervene. He wanted to see who knew the Heimlich Maneuver. His theatrics were masterful. While everyone was standing in line piling cold cuts on their plates, he began to sputter, turn red, and clutch his throat. He spit the legs of a rubber spider from his mouth, and then acted as if the insect's body was obstructing his airway. Holding his breath, he fell to his knees as he turned deep crimson.

No one moved to help him. One of the nurses turned to the person standing next to her and muttered, "Good. I hope he chokes to death, so that we don't have to listen to any more of his lectures." Of course, she recognized that his choking was a prank, but her tone of voice revealed that my teaching companion had not yet endeared himself to his students.

The next day, everyone was sitting on the beach listening to another lecture when my doctor friend fell off his seat and landed softly in the sand. He immediately turned pale, began to sweat, and complained of horrible pain in his knee. He claimed that he couldn't bend his leg and asked for assistance. Ten onlookers didn't believe him, so they headed for their rafts and shoved off into the river, voting that he once again was attempting to trip them up with a simulation. Three of us, a male dentist, a female nurse, and me, stayed behind because we sensed that something actually was wrong.

My friend told me that he couldn't straighten his knee and that he wasn't faking it. Sweat beaded on his brow from the pain. I tried to move him and he moaned in agony. My diagnosis was that he had a small piece of cartilage stuck in the joint and that straightening his leg was pinching it. We needed to do something.

An evacuation was possible, but expensive. I rummaged through my medical kit and found some morphine, but was dismayed to observe that in my haste to pack, I had neglected to bring the injectable antidote that would reverse the harmful side effects of the narcotic. If my friend suffered difficulty breathing or a sudden drop in blood pressure, I wouldn't be able to help him.

I offered him a choice—a three thousand dollar evacuation or an attempt to fix his knee. I tried to lighten the situation by telling him that I could inject, but that if he stopped breathing, he'd be in a deep pickle, since I preferred to not do mouth-to-mouth on him. I turned to the dentist and nurse, who concurred by shaking their heads from side to side. The suffering doctor said, "Go for it." I administered the drug and watched my friend fall quickly asleep. The dentist held countertraction on the victim's upper thigh while I forcefully twisted and rocked his lower leg until I felt a "pop," which signified that the trapped cartilage had exited the knee joint. As soon as that happened, I noticed that his leg bent and extended with ease. We quickly fashioned a cylindrical splint from a kayaker's life jacket, taped it in place, and waited for our patient to awaken. All the while, the nurse held his hand and pressed a cold washcloth to his forehead.

He drifted out of his drug-induced slumber, and mumbled that his suffering was over. For the next half hour, he continued to groggily repeat his thanks to the nurse, who had done nothing more than wield a cool cloth and offer a few words of encouragement. Still, that was all my patient could remember. He wasn't interested in my resourcefulness or technical proficiency, but rather in the humane ministrations of the person who had soothed him during his time of need.

The point should never be lost on anyone who will care for a patient. All of the high-technology stuff is fantastic, but what patients really want is to be cared for, to have a demonstration of caring, to feel like they are family when it comes to attention and concern. That is their need and that is what they deserve.

The same holds true for customers. Certainly, they are sensitive to price and service, but if you dig down deep, you will discover that each and every one of them expects personal attention. What is "caring?" Caring is courtesy, respect, advice, gratitude, and compassion. It isn't unqualified approval of bad business decisions or mistakes that derive from laziness or inadequate cerebration. Rather, it is a commitment to personalize the impersonal, to make every person feel that he or she is valued as an individual, and to always put yourself in the other person's position.

Learn How to Triage

In a disaster or mass casualty situation, victims are assigned to different categories by the process of "triage," or sorting. Persons with minor injuries are segregated from those who are seriously injured, who are in turn separated from those who are near death. The rationale is that in a situation with limited medical resources, people requiring a disproportionate amount of attention and supplies with little chance for survival should be left unattended in favor of helping those who might have a reasonable shot at survival while consuming less resources. In this manner, judgments are made that will lead to the maximal number of functioning survivors. This is in contrast to the situation in which there are limitless resources and everything can be done for a catastrophically injured person in hope that a near miracle might occur. The most experienced individual is assigned the task of triage, because he should have the best insight into who can be saved and who cannot.

Unless you have limitless resources and can continuously apply them to all magnitudes of problems, you also need to triage in certain business situations. This requires a thorough understanding of your personnel, financial situation, priorities, and ability to sustain specific losses. On the opportunity side, it requires assessment of relative risks and rewards. This generally relates to the application of resources to different business units and growth situations, which is still a question of putting effort and money in one direction at the expense of another.

Inherent in the ability to triage is to recognize certain death, or in the context of business, inevitable failure. One needs to be able to recognize when the loss of a client is inevitable, and let that client go. This may go against the grain of many, who believe that you should never give up under any circumstance, and that all situations are potentially salvageable. This just isn't true. You need to understand the metrics of your business sufficiently well to be able to tell when enough is enough. This can be extraordinarily painful when your organization is the cause of the failure and you haven't been able to rectify the situation, but while you are resuscitating a hopeless situation, think about whether all of the resources you have diverted would be better focused upon ten other situations that are at risk for a similar fate if you don't get them back on track.

Finally, you should remember that triage is a dynamic process. Unless a business unit or situation was deemed to be in excellent health, you must come back to it at intervals to see whether something has now arisen that requires your attention. You can never become less concerned until the patient is completely healed.

Every Company Is a Service Company

Medical care is delivered as service to a customer, the patient. Every doctor, therefore, is in the service business. A great way to improve is to observe who is successful, study what they do, and adopt the methods that make sense. The second entrant always benefits when there is local expertise from which to learn. Whether it's bedside manner, pricing, availability, or referral patterns, it's good to know what has worked for others.

What about the converse—medical practices that have failed? The same holds true. Learn from them. I'll tell you the most common reason that someone leaves his or her doctor. It's because the person doesn't feel like the doctor listens any more. It's because they've *both* become numbers, and are no longer honored as unique individuals. The spirit of service has been eliminated. Even the perception of waning interest by a doctor can be enough to cause a patient to defect.

If you don't want your company to lose its service edge, *then study the best service organizations.* These don't need to be nonprofits. Many nonprofits become complacent, because their customers don't hold them to the same level of accountability. I suggest looking at the great finance, transportation, and retail corporations. Pick a company that receives high marks from its peers for the following characteristics:

1. The customer truly comes first.
2. Communication between employees and with customers is guaranteed.
3. Prolonged wait times for service are unacceptable.
4. Prices are fair.
5. The senior managers are in place to solve problems.
6. Client service representatives make the customers feel important.
7. There is a culture of learning.
8. There is money set aside for research and development to support all of the above.

Service is about feeling good when you can do something for someone. It is never delivered with a begrudging attitude. A good example is someone who does a great job at a call center. Whether it's a technician on the phone that helps untangle a software tangle or a nurse that guides you through treatment of your child's fever, the enthusiasm comes across with impact equal to the message. When I first encounter a patient, I make it a point to let the person know that I'm there to help, and that I'll stick with him or her until we find a solution. That reassurance and the patient's confidence in my ability to focus is as much a part of the cure as any operation or drug.

Always Roll the Patient Over and Look at His Back

It's human nature to focus on the obvious. In emergency medicine, some of the first things we learn are the "ABCs," which, as mentioned earlier, stand for airway, breathing, and circulation. Everyone becomes very focused on the serious problems, as well they should, before moving on to a more detailed examination of the entire patient.

In all of the commotion, when you're putting in tubes and infusing lifesaving drugs, it's easy to forget to examine every nook and cranny. However, there's a good reason why a thorough examination is essential, even if you believe the major problem is obvious. You must never forget to roll the patient over and look at his back. It's easy to miss a second stab wound if you don't look for it carefully.

One night, a call rang down from the paramedics that they were transporting a drowning victim, who was cold and now in full cardiac arrest. No one knew why he had fallen in the water, but it was obvious that he was nearly dead, with a faint pulse and no breathing. If he had been found on the street, he would have been declared dead, but since he was pulled from the water and was extremely cold, there was a chance that he was a victim of hypothermia. We initiated a full-court press to resuscitate him, which lasted for more than three hours and tied up everyone in the E.R.

The course of the resuscitation made no sense, because he should have rewarmed more quickly. I undressed him and looked at his back, and everywhere else, I thought. I didn't find anything. Ultimately, when nothing improved, the patient was pronounced dead. The next day, I received a telephone call from the coroner, who started the conversation by praising me.

"Say Paul, I read the medical report. That was quite a resuscitation."

"Yes, it was."

"So, you really went after this guy pretty hard. What were you thinking?" I knew the coroner pretty well, and by the tone of his voice, he had something on his mind.

"He was pretty cold. We thought we might get him back."

"Yeah. I figured it was something like that. You really threw the book at him." Now I knew I was in trouble.

"Sure did. Didn't get any response, though. I would've thought we'd see something. Guess he was too far gone."

There was a pregnant pause, and then he let me in on his little secret. "You know, I was wondering something." I didn't say anything. "You didn't by chance notice that little bullet hole behind his ear, did you?"

It was easy to see how we could miss the bullet hole. The victim had come in cold and soaking wet, with his hair matted down. Still, the coroner taught us all a lesson.

The man had a fatal injury that we hadn't detected, and we wasted a solid three hours and a tremendous effort in a futile exercise.

When an employee comes into my business office in a panic with a certain explanation for a problem—the equivalent of a diagnosis—I make the assumption that there has to be another cause. It's usually a fairly quick process to investigate the obvious and affirm whether or not a solution is as straightforward as advertised, but even after the major difficulty is addressed, you must go back and perform a complete analysis and be certain that you haven't missed the less obvious, or even obscure, contributor.

People are quick to find an easy solution, because it takes less effort and seems to eliminate the problem. They gravitate toward working in areas in which they have comfort and interest, and often won't tackle new and complex situations without being prodded. Often, the long-term effects of such an approach can't be measured until a period of time when other confounding variables don't contribute to muddying the waters. While it's counterproductive to have everyone in your organization be obsessive-compulsive, someone needs to understand the important protocols and be certain that essential managerial processes are not foregone for the easy and obvious repair jobs. Otherwise, you will spend many extra hours fixing situations that should have been fixed right the first time, or left as they are.

Treat the Patient, Not the Numbers

Doctors order lots of tests, and most of the results are numbers. Sometimes those numbers are essential for decision making, but many of them are noise. The problem with medical noise is that you are obligated to react to it. Is it a gunshot or just backfire from a car exhaust? Is the patient's potassium level really dangerously high, or did the lab just let the specimen sit around too long?

The numbers may not make sense. When I have a small child sitting in front of me after treatment for an asthma attack, smiling and breathing easily, is it possible that I'm missing something? The laboratory result indicates a severe metabolic abnormality, but it doesn't make sense. If I react to what's written on the slip of paper, the drugs I might use are potentially dangerous. Furthermore, if I treat a patient with normal potassium as if she is suffering from high potassium, I will create a situation of low potassium, and that's not good.

Evidence-based medicine has arisen as the current clinical method in response to a more subjective approach that has been shown to drive up costs. Decision trees with statistics and percentages have been formulated to allow physicians to proceed expeditiously to proper diagnoses and therapies. But any other cookbook approach to a complex discipline can suggest an intervention that is wrong, given the total picture. The most flagrant example of this is when the laboratory reports numbers that don't make sense. In response to this form

179

of medical error, the teaching is "treat the patient, not the numbers."

The most prevalent business expression is "make the numbers." Profit, loss, and margin drive all manner of financial ratios that ultimately determine the success or failure of a business. When a business is in trouble, sometimes the problem is reflected in these calculations, and sometimes it isn't. The arithmetic is the effect, and behavior is the cause. An errant financial result doesn't necessarily identify the problem for me, so if I apply a quick fix, I may miss the root cause. The most common approach to a bad outcome is to cut expenses, but that's only a housekeeping maneuver that lets you see where you can do something more constructive.

The most important application of this advice is to be critical in your interpretation of data when they don't make sense. A perfect example of this is in the assessment of information gathered from focus groups. They can often lead you to conclusions that seem sensible in the seclusion of a conference room, but are irrelevant in the real world. In medicine, new drugs are introduced though Phase I, Phase II, and Phase III clinical trials. These trials determine if a drug can be administered safely with intended effects and without untoward side effects. They are performed on real patients in real clinical settings, because rabbits and rats are not people. The same holds true for your theories about how new ideas will work in your business. I wouldn't trust a focus group to be the final decision maker in matters of taste. There have been too many colossal consumer design predictive errors to lead me to skip the real-world test market.

Ultimately, Satisfaction Drives Everything

Health care is undergoing reformation in the U.S., stimulated by rising costs and the legislative imperative to do something. The real truth is that in a system historically driven by a cost-plus, fee-for-service mentality, there has never been the alignment of incentives necessary to promote appropriate utilization.

Prospective payment, health maintenance organizations, and capitation as payment methods for medical services have evolved with astounding rapidity in response to projections that predict insolvency of health-care entitlement programs. The impact of these financial structures upon the quality of health care is debated. We are early in the cycle of data collection to support or refute any contention about long-term effects upon patients, providers, and institutions that comprise our health-care system. And for sure, with each federal election cycle, we will see tinkering with benefits and government support, issued in the name of the electorate, but largely (in my opinion) perpetrated to obtain votes.

Fortunately, constructive patterns are emerging. Consumers are demanding information and they don't like to be constrained. As far as health care goes, we all appreciate the right care at the right place by the right person at the right price, but we want input into the definition of

Paul S. Auerbach, M.D.

some of these "rights." If controlling costs means removing personal freedom and eliminating choice, this smacks of monopoly, which sets off all sorts of alarms.

I believe that there is something different about health care, as opposed to, say, public transportation. The type of vulnerability created by an illness and the personal relationship developed between patient and physician are different from needing to travel on a bus and desiring the right to converse with the driver. Consumers should not view health care as a commodity. Price is important, but probably not the overriding concern in most people's minds. It's the rare person who doesn't want the best possible medicine delivered by the most highly skilled person. Health care is highly personal, and implies relationships that transcend the business transaction.

This places a greater burden on the health-care provider. Expected to be as efficient as possible, the physician must also be communicative, compassionate, patient, skillful, and current. He or she must have access to recent literature and knowledgeable specialists, and to never exceed personal limits of education or competence. Errors are subject to extreme scrutiny and peer review, and there is little tolerance for late, defective, or incorrect activity. Reimbursement for many physicians is dropping like a stone—consider the fact that the hourly compensation to an emergency physician is less than that paid to a landscape architect who suggests what shrubs you should plant on your patio. I am not arguing that a lesser standard should therefore be applied to doctors because their compensation is diminishing. The sacred trust and high expectations are appropriate and what make the practice of medicine so special. I am merely making an observation.

If we assume that over time, scientific data, public debate, market forces, motivated providers, ethics committees, and government regulations will remove the most significant excesses from health-care costs so that the delivery system will be appropriately priced, what becomes the next driver of change? Many pundits proclaim that it will be quality, but I think they're wrong. I believe that the next wave to carry the health-care delivery system will be customer satisfaction. This is because quality is too difficult to measure with imperfect information systems, there is much disagreement about the definition of what constitutes quality, and because real power resides with patients, not with statistics. The Holy Grail of medical information, an integrated electronic patient record, isn't here yet. I predict that it will be at least a decade before all of the disparate information systems are configured to talk to each other and providers are persuaded that they are sufficiently confidential and user-friendly to adopt on a wide scale. If the past is indicative of the future, the competitive nature of physicians, and the corporations that increasingly control them, will direct outcome data to achieve market advantage, which does not necessarily coincide with public health.

Consumers, on the other hand, have numerous advocates unwilling to accept the status quo. While employees would love to base health-care provider decisions on outcomes, physician profiles, and the like, these data are new and imperfect, and in many cases, difficult to obtain. It's much easier to talk to your neighbor and ask, "How long did you wait?," "How well were you treated?," and, "Would you use this doctor or hospital again?" Such inquiries drive to the heart of the doctor-patient relationship. All the smarts in the world notwithstanding, the doctor who cannot communicate with patients or who evokes an image of dispassion rather than compassion will drive patients to seek care elsewhere. Customers demand customer service. Patients are customers, any way you cut it. Doctors who don't recognize that they are part of a service industry will become the "dinosaur docs" of the future. In an era when increasing technology and shifts to alternative delivery methods will diminish the number of doctors necessary to manage a given population, I wouldn't count on an aloof approach being viable.

It's fascinating that in the world of widgets and mass production, where it's important that your personal computer arrives on time and works properly out of the box (but let's face it, nobody suffers or drops dead if it doesn't), customer service has been a mantra for decades. If you go into Nordstrom's and ask for a certain pair of shoes, and the salesperson says they don't have it, don't intend to have it, and doesn't volunteer to order it or help you find it somewhere else, will you ever go back there? If his supervisor hears from you about this episode, how long will that employee last?

This is a situation where the doctor can learn from the corporate executive and vice versa. For the doctor, it's no longer a given that patients are captive and that service doesn't matter. HMOs are experiencing consumer backlash associated with loss of choice and limitation of services. Employers and health plans are scrambling to reintroduce choice. In a sea of paperwork, the harried and inconsiderate physician will lose patients to the provider who takes an extra moment and connects with his patients in an interactive way. Health plans that unduly burden their providers and regiment them in such a way as to compromise the doctor-patient relationship will inevitably fall prey to the programs that figure out how to preserve the essential interactions. Remember that the costs are going to get squeezed out. It's inevitable. Then, the spoils will fall to the best and the best loved. I suggest that doctors look to successful service industries, such as certain airlines, to become masters at customer service. If you are a physician reading this and are compelled to utter, "Medicine has nothing to do with airplanes. It's different," I would reply, "No it isn't. Your challenge is to be a wonderful doctor and to adapt to what the patients are saying they expect of you. More often than not, they have a choice, and their choices will increase in the future, so you'd better shape up. As a doctor, you are still special, but get over yourself."

If you're a corporate executive, then I think you should reflect upon the doctor-patient scenario and try to recognize what is so special about that relationship.

Paul S. Auerbach, M.D.

When it works well, it's unparalleled in any industry. It contains insight, long-term trust, the ability to adapt in a crisis, and bonds forged out of mutual dependencies, successes, and failures. Despite the occasional brilliance of a solo practitioner, it is increasingly an art practiced in teams, multidisciplinary by design and necessity. Applied to a customer-product-service paradigm, it emphasizes the essential nature of understanding the capabilities of your operatives and their ability to guide an enterprise through an unpredictable and stormy path. It's a no-excuse environment through which a person can express energies that truly benefit another human being. It is this last element that should be replicable in any corporate enterprise. When persons believe that what they do truly makes the world better for someone, it adds credibility to the company that cannot be provided in any other mind frame.

Know When You Have Time for Complexity, and When You Must Keep It Simple

Teaching effectively in a busy environment is difficult, particularly when an error is unacceptable. This is compounded in matters of medicine, as patients will not tolerate mistakes made in the name of education. Multiply this dilemma tenfold in a busy E.R., where there are additional constraints of time. The number one responsibility of a faculty physician in a busy E.R. is to keep things moving. The patients don't want to wait, the nurses want the place cleared out, and you have to move each patient along promptly to make room for the patients that follow.

However, no patient is concerned with the fate of any other, so each expects to be seen next. The consultant specialists rarely are willing to disrupt their routines in order to facilitate the situation. The health plan authorization clerks at the other end of the phone line would just as soon deny everything, as their incentives are driven off decreasing utilization, so they put you on hold only to come back and argue about how this particular kidney stone should be treated at an office appointment in two weeks.

Forget about the niceties. Once you get past all of the usual aphorisms about quality of care and patient satisfaction, you get to the meat of the operation, which is keeping the place moving. The definition of unscheduled care is that you never know when the next busload of hemophiliacs will arrive. You must constantly push the system to maximal efficiency and the E.R. to your fantasy, which is a condition of vacancy. If you let your guard down and the patients begin to pile up, you will then have to commit the ultimate sin, which is to "close" the E.R.

When you're in charge and it's obvious what needs to be done to keep everything moving forward, make rapid decisions and expect everyone to do precisely as you say. The more complicated the environment, the more likely that simple solutions will suffice. However, expect everyone to be enamored of complexity. When you have the ability to cut to a solution, it may take everyone by surprise, so offer full explanations. The skill of a senior manager is to be able to see a straight path and to walk it. When the E.R. is packed and there are fifty patients in the waiting room, someone has to be unpopular and get the consultants to respond, the nurses to room patients faster, and the house officers to curtail lengthy individual work-ups in deference to the needs of the aggregate patient population.

You will recognize problems in your business that require quick solutions, and should be inclined to take a direct path. Your employees may wish to follow a more circuitous route, not believing that a simple approach can be as accurate as one that is more intricately crafted. It becomes your responsibility to see that the group gets where it needs to go in the time frame that's appropriate for your business needs. While it's always a laudable goal to teach while you work, you must make certain that things move along, even if it sacrifices certain opportunities for education. Patient care comes first.

Alarms Are Frightening

Technology can be intimidating to nontechnophiles. When a loud noise blares on a medical monitor, it sounds like a burglar alarm. A loose electrode taped to someone's chest can cause the squiggly green line on the heart tracing to go "flat line," and everybody knows what *that* means. So now you're a patient in the E.R., wired from every orifice, and a shrill blast sounds from the big metal box attached to your intravenous tubing. The nurse doesn't even turn around. Are you dying? Shouldn't someone run over and fix something?

Sometimes the alarm means something and sometimes it doesn't. The manufacturers have the darned things set to go off if someone sneezes on the other side of the room. We all know that there are a dozen false alarms to every one that means anything, but what does the patient know? Not much, unless we've told them. The technology has to be tailored to the customer, so each patient requires an explanation about what to expect.

Consider the complexity of what you are trying to accomplish. If automation is a solution, be prepared. Everyone should know how to accomplish the same task manually if necessary. It's nice to have medicine pumps with timers, but that doesn't remove the obligation to know how to count drops and keep time with a wristwatch. Furthermore, knowing what to do with a false alarm is just as important as what to do when the real thing happens. When the numbers don't add up, everyone tends to panic before they remember to re-count by an alternate method, and perform a reconciliation.

Also, if you don't speak the language, get a translator who is technically proficient. When I deal with a patient who speaks a foreign language, it's not enough to have a family member translate. If the translator doesn't understand medicine in *any* language, my message is almost certainly going to suffer in the translation. The same holds true when trying to transmit technical information. You have to be able to talk across languages and across disciplines.

Get rid of the acronyms first. "The SAH arrived post-MI and was nearly DOA. I DC'd her ACE-inhibitor QAM in preference for a BID and PRN beta-blocker PO to keep her from losing her DTRs and becoming a DNR." Wonderful. Try to have a frightened family member translate that. When you are trying to work across disciplines, particularly when the jargon becomes technical, try to simplify everything, and spell it out.

Make the Routine Important and Extraordinary

When I was a senior medical student, I discussed career options with a famous chest surgeon. When I asked him how he had chosen his specialty, he answered that he could get just as excited about putting in a pacemaker as he could about performing difficult open heart surgery. Furthermore, he considered it his responsibility as a leader to instill that same enthusiasm in every member of his team. No operation, if it was his responsibility, was trivial or boring.

That's easier said than done. In the E.R., it's difficult to equate a routine strep throat with a ruptured spleen in terms of acuity, diagnostic challenge, or necessity for rapid action. Emergency medicine has its "pacemakers," but I for one do not gravitate to them. However, that's *my* problem. A patient with a tension headache won't suffer in the long term like a victim of appendicitis, but suffering is in the eye of the beholder. Who's to tell the small child with a "hot ear" that he's any less deserving than a motorcycle accident victim with a broken leg? Furthermore, can I ever suggest to a young doctor in training that "boring" patients deserve less than their full attention? Of course not. It's my obligation to make the less interesting more appealing, both intellectually and emotionally. The routine should become extraordinary.

This also holds true for the support staff. It's hard for a registration clerk to get excited about shuffling the paperwork faster when the motivation is meeting a quota or finishing a shift. However, if the clerk understands how efficient registration leads someone to care more quickly, acquires critical information that might be missed, or uncovers a thorny social situation for which an intervention can be made, then the workplace becomes much more satisfying. The ordinary paperwork process becomes an extraordinary inquiry and documentation effort that contributes to the care of the patient.

Another trick for adding an element of importance to what might otherwise seem routine is to point out that all is not what it seems. A simple rash can be a rare infectious disease; an aching shoulder a manifestation of an occult tumor, rather than soreness from a weekend of golf. Epidemics are propagated out of lack of observation, which can be attributed to the untrained or unmotivated eye. If the only perceptive eyes are those of the most highly skilled scientists and physicians, enormous opportunities will be lost.

Imagine the satisfaction of people who never expect to work their way up, when they are given a chance to contribute, to make a difference. When their work becomes extraordinary, they begin to appreciate the same potential and satisfaction as the experts.

Get this started by letting everybody in the company understand the relationships, and how each activity is important to another. Communication is mostly what is lacking when people get bored or start doing redundant work, because they don't understand how important it is to be coordinated and to look continuously for improvements. Layer some incentives on top of communication, and you begin to give people a predictable reason to excel. If you can't get excited about what happens a couple of levels below you, then assign the program to somebody who is there and incentivized to look at happy faces.

Rework Is Never as Good as Getting It Right the First Time

On occasion, I've walked into a patient's room and discovered that an unsupervised medical student has incorrectly repaired a wound. I must now apologize to the patient, convince him to endure another procedure, and then remove all of the stitches. This represents a failure at multiple levels: my failure to have impressed upon the student the importance of obtaining appropriate guidance, failure of the nursing staff to bird-dog the student, and failure of the student to respect the patient. The E.R. has now lost the patient's confidence, increased its liability if there's a complication, and been rendered inefficient. All of this because a young person didn't think to let someone look over his shoulder and make sure he was getting it right the first time.

We learn from mistakes. A good teacher knows how to apply a guiding hand while leading a student to intellectual and procedural independence. It's a delicate balance. A significant part of the process is setting boundaries and enforcing rules. One thing's for certain— patients expect their doctors to get it right the first time, and they don't want to be guinea pigs. In a teaching hospital, a decent explanation leads most patients to cooperate, so long as there is genuine supervision.

In a business, your employees have to understand when to ask for help. I tell all of my medical students and residents the same things that I tell my charges in a business setting—I will only become angry if they don't ask for help when they need it, and that I don't like surprises. What I mean by the latter is that I want to know when they're having difficulty, because I'm supposed to be there to help them, and I often can't do that after the failure has been completed. Although I appreciate people who show initiative and don't want to bother me with stupid questions, I'd rather take the time and help someone with the first stitch than have to go back and take them all out. This philosophy works best if it can be promoted without becoming micromanagement that makes everyone afraid of his own shadow. One helpful approach is to broach the level of participation with the customer. Let everyone know the qualifications of the team, so that trainees are clearly identified and always supported by someone who can vouch for their integrity. This is the perspective of an operations person. A CEO operating from the "30,000-foot level" may be more content to let the business move along without supervision, but there had better be *somebody* minding the store.

Changing Information Systems Sounds Better Than It Really Is

The Holy Grail of informatics in medicine is the longitudinal electronic medical record. This, we are told, will allow every doctor in the world to communicate with every other doctor. Medicine will be based on perfect information, unnecessary tests and interventions will be eliminated, and errors will be prevented. The current situation is a Tower of Babel of paper records, to which anyone sporting a believable doctor disguise can have access. On the other hand, the electronic medical record will be secure and integrated, so that a doctor in Des Moines can review a record from Los Angeles, instantaneously, in confidence, and with total precision.

The problem is that it's not that simple. There have been hundreds of millions of dollars invested in developing proprietary solutions, in order to replace the paper

Tower with an electronic Tower. Furthermore, some health-care organizations and doctors believe that because they know how to take care of patients, they also should know how to develop software. Not true. The mentality that drives hard business decisions and gets Version 1.0 of software out the door does not prevail in the stereotypical groups of physicians working on projects. I can guarantee that competitive advantages in health-care organizations won't be maintained by failing at software development.

Year 2000 notwithstanding, there are precious few reasons to switch software every time the "next generation" comes along. How much time can be saved, how many dollars conserved, how many hospital days eliminated, how many patients cured who might otherwise have met their demise? If we didn't introduce a single new word processing program, spread sheet, or database, would the science of medicine be impeded? Would the physiology of mankind suffer? Would we be overcome by undetected plagues? I doubt it. The truth is, if we declared a moratorium on competition fueled by advertising the "latest and greatest," the man-hours saved and financial resources that could be devoted to pure research and health-care delivery would likely be more than tripled. Market forces may control runaway health-care costs, but these same forces make us compete on absurd playing fields, where scientists are dragged into deliberations about the strategic advantage of push technology promulgated by drug companies via the Internet, rather than in what ways their technical expertise can be deployed to assist developing nations stricken with famine and communicable diseases.

The return on investment going from a manual to an automated environment can be measured, but the incremental advantages after the major transition are more often fluff than substance. The buzzword "integration" keeps the machinery of software startups rolling, but what's so integrated about health care? Illness is generally episodic, and once a chronic condition becomes evident, a single provider can coordinate care. I would agree that information transfer is generally inadequate, but the solution lies in the hands of the consumer, not the provider. Who cares more about continuity and lack of error, the patient or the doctor? Who suffers physically, emotionally, and financially when there is a less than desirable outcome?

So, what are the compelling reasons to develop or purchase new computers or software? It needs to make a process measurably more efficient. There needs to be a quantified financial benefit. A desirable outcome of the transition, whether or not profits increase, must be articulated. The transition should facilitate a more agile position for the recipients of the new program. It should serve a true business need, and not be change for the sake of change.

Exclusivity can be a strategic advantage, but only if your competitors would use the software if it became available to them. What I mean by this is the old adage,

"You can lead a horse to water, but you can't make it drink." An electronic medical record purchased off the shelf and with minimal customization is better than an elaborate, full on bells-and-whistles version that costs you three years' profits and that no one else would ever use. You should design for the lowest common denominator of technical expertise in your organization, unless you can assure that the chain will not break because of a weak user link. Anticipate subversives, who didn't want the change, didn't invent it, and may actually try to sabotage it. Look carefully at how critical information is transferred in your organization; it is at these junctures that you will find the most compelling need for spending money on information systems. Using technology to "get rid of people" can eliminate human error and therefore defective work products, but it is a dehumanizing posture that can get you into trouble with your customers if you are in a service business.

Leave Microsurgery to the Microsurgeon

There are many reasons why doctors refer patients to specialists. The most valid is that the patient's condition requires special expertise. For instance, a patient comes to the E.R. A single bullet entered his palm and exited the top of his hand. There's a small puncture at the entrance wound, but the entire top of the hand is a gaping hole with a hideous tangle of torn tendons and ripped tissues. This is clearly beyond my expertise. So, I administer pain medicine to keep the patient comfortable, antibiotics to help prevent infection, apply a dressing to control bleeding, and call a hand surgeon.

Once you've made the decision that you're going to delegate the care of your patient to another physician, should you continue to examine the wound, to see what else you can find? Should you attempt to match the ends of the severed tendons, and line everything up for the surgeon? Should you begin to trim away skin and bone fragments? The answer is a resounding, "No!" At this point, you are beginning to move into unfamiliar territory, and although your intentions are good, you become increasingly likely to make a mistake.

What if you're a retired hand surgeon, and now working in the E.R. as a generalist emergency physician? You used to take care of stuff like this all the time. Should you therefore begin to manage this wound yourself, because it will take a little while for the hand surgeon to come to the hospital? Again, unless you can show that the patient would otherwise have a worse outcome, the answer is, "No."

Once you have engaged someone in a critical task, let him or her do it. You have chosen a specialist either because you needed their expertise, because you have the expertise but don't have the time to take care of the problem yourself, or because it is your policy in this situation to defer to another physician. It isn't fair to the person given the assignment to have to adjust to your well-meaning, but potentially complicating, ministrations. Abandon your compulsive nature or desire to impress the crowd. Accept your new role graciously, and learn from your consultant.

If you delegate down, avoid being a micromanager, unless it's an intentional effort to teach or you have a well-delineated role as a team member. This is a difficult concept for senior managers, many of whom have migrated to executive roles from former careers as staff persons. Nothing is more annoying to a junior person trying to get his or her work done, and to establish some self-confidence in the process, than a meddler. Even worse is the phenomenon of dueling meddlers. For instance, dual reporting is fraught with emotional hazard. If there has to be a hierarchy, keep it simple, and let it be clearly known who is responsible for which decisions. Discussions and creative activities are great team processes, but situations of great intensity (such as repairing a difficult hand wound) are better managed with a focused approach by a well supported, solo practitioner.

Listen and Learn

In an encounter with a patient, there is opportunity for both service and learning. The former is obvious, because that's why the patient came to see you in the first place. The latter can be more difficult, because of the relationship, barriers to receptivity on the part of the physician, and precarious cultural bridges. This communication challenge holds a major key for job satisfaction—namely, learning while you work. The time constraints imposed by managed care have introduced three major dissatisfiers into health care: decreased compensation, an assembly line mentality, and unhappy patients. The latter two have stifled many of the interactions that were possible when physicians felt truly connected to their patients. In the E.R., it's always been difficult to get connected, and yet the openings for relationship building exist nonetheless.

When you *listen* to patients, you *learn* from them. You learn about the varieties of ways that a person reacts to a disease, about the nuances of signs and symptoms, about their work and families, how the health-care system has treated them, and their hopes and fears. When you *listen* to consultants, you *learn* from them. You learn about new therapies and services, how the hospital works, and how you are perceived in the workplace. It is this learning, from your patients and your profession, that keeps the job interesting. There are moments of excitement in what you do repetitively, but I think satisfaction is more profoundly generated in learning. The glorious part of medicine is that it can be a constant source of professional renewal, if you can avoid becoming set in your ways.

When I look at pictures of laborers, they are never smiling. They're toiling, and I would wager that most of them are bored. I can accept the fact that this is an acceptable state for people who aren't highly skilled and therefore paid minimum wage. But what about you? Midlevel managers and executives should rarely be unhappy, and if so, it certainly shouldn't be because they're bored. Think back to your school days. If you were bored, you either weren't challenged, you had a lousy teacher, or you were genuinely uninterested in the subject. An observant someone should have intervened. All three circumstances apply to the business situation.

People stay on the job longer and are more productive when they're engaged. When they *listen* to customers, they *learn* from them. They come to know their preferences, buying patterns, product criticisms, and level of satisfaction with service. When you *listen* to your employees, you *learn* from them. You discover how they feel about their work, whether they are happy, what they believe might be improved, how they think you're doing as a manager. Most important, you can determine if they are learning anything. If they're not learning or teaching, they are becoming emotional robots, and unless that is what you or they desire, they'll find a way to exit your company.

Reevaluate Your Processes and Desired Outcomes Constantly

Solving one problem relieves the pain in one area and allows another pain to break through. Consider the patient with a broken neck, which may be only minimally painful, who also has a broken ankle, which can cause pain sufficient to cause delirium. Improper manip-

Paul S. Auerbach, M.D.

ulation of the neck injury can damage the spinal cord and cause paralysis, while improper manipulation of the ankle may cause some delayed arthritis, but could never be life threatening. When a patient comes into the E.R., he may not recognize his neck injury, since his focus is upon the intense ankle pain. After you realign the foot and put the ankle in a splint, the pain is usually somewhat relieved. It may be only at this time that the patient notices the pain in his neck. By creating some relief in one area, there is now the opportunity to recognize pain in another. The evaluation of the patient should begin all over again, and the focus of the investigation shift appropriately to the areas of greatest concern.

But this is all without any intentional diversions. Most patients do their best to direct their doctors to the true cause of their difficulties, because they desire relief. It may not be so straightforward in your business, because asking for help with a problem may be construed as a sign of weakness. This is foolish, but it's common. Therefore, the best way to keep drilling down into a situation in order to achieve a comprehensive understanding is to find a problem, fix it, and then see what else becomes apparent after the solution is applied. If your new sales and marketing plan brings you the growth rate you desire, but your current customers are still not satisfied, move along to the next problem, and fix it. Seek confirmation from your customers that you have satisfied their concerns, and then ask if there are additional problems. When the response gets down to nitpicking (or your patient wants to show you a small scratch on their elbow), you can discharge the problem.

Hitting a Fastball Is Timing, Not Power

This speaks to the preparation phase that precedes execution. When I teach young doctors how to insert an intravenous catheter into the vein of a patient, I emphasize that the insertion can be easier than it looks if the event is seen as merely one point in the continuum of a process. Most beginners are fixated on the moment when the needle enters the skin. You can see it in the trembling of their hands. The less confident the operator, the more his hands shake and the less likely that the procedure will be successful.

The same is true of a hitter in the batter's box. Perhaps he is worried about getting struck by a fastball or worried about the coach's criticism if he strikes out. Fear takes away the batter's focus so that he can't concentrate on the elements that lead to a hit. Line up your feet properly. Position the bat. Lift your elbow. Keep your eye on the ball. Step into the pitch. *Not* "Get ready to duck. Everybody's watching me. I hope I don't strike out."

A good batting coach tells his players that hitting a fastball is timing, not power. A fluid stroke to aim the hit, not just strike the ball, is the art of batting. Skinny arms can lash a fastball just as effectively as muscular limbs when the motion is correct and the moments of force are perfect.

It's no different slipping a catheter into a patient. Success lies in a conscientious preparation and follow-through. The formula for failure is to be in a rush, to have your mind on other things, to be under pressure, or to be showing off. Teaching creates a certain imperative for successful completion, but this can be mitigated by even more attention to detail.

Success is most often achieved when you don't need to separate the insertion into its component parts. The motion is smooth and effortless once you appreciate the rhythm of what you are doing. When you become good, repetition can make you nearly flawless, and your reputation grows. When that happens, you get asked to insert catheters when others encounter difficulty. You are assigned the "tough sticks," the people with dwindled and scarred veins, the small children with tiny and imperceptible blood vessels. You accept these challenges, further improve your technique, and become a master. This becomes a cycle of success, and your peers and patients are enormously appreciative, because you have helped them.

In making your company work, you need to understand all the working parts, but if the coordination isn't right, swinging harder won't get a hit. If you are threading your way through a difficult negotiation or labor dispute, in addition to identifying the key points, you must understand how they link together, and how to move smoothly between concepts. Pushing and pulling are part of a continuum, and effective coaching is a process

of reminders during the game, not fundamentals teaching in the heat of the battle. Your team needs to thoroughly understand how you would have them do things
before the event, so that you can confine your participation to adjustments. They need to understand your
thoughts on integration, so that they can integrate for
themselves. The faster the pitch or the more tortuous the
vein, the greater the need to have impeccable timing and
motion. From a corporate perspective, this need be no
more complicated than making sure that the left hand
knows what the right hand is doing. We spend a lot of
time creating teams that consist of multiple individuals
within a department, or divisions within a company.
What we forget is that *an individual is a team unto himself,
who needs to recognize his diversity of capabilities and skills,
and learn how to coordinate them effectively for a best personal effort.*

The Only People Who Make Money Capturing Eyeballs Are Ophthalmologists

To launch the commercial Internet age, there was a gold
rush. Like the Forty-Niners, everyone staked their
claims and hoped there were nuggets below the surface.
The shakeout thus far has demonstrated emphatically
that most of what glitters can't be converted to currency,
and that (again), it's expensive to move your family out
West in search of fame and fortune. The opening mantra
was "capturing eyeballs." Build it and they will come.

From my medical experience, I can affirm that the only people who make money capturing eyeballs are ophthalmologists.

When you write your next business plan for an Internet company, be sure you put in something about how you're going to make money. But leave out advertising revenues and donations. Don't even mutter the word "eyeballs." The Internet will ultimately be successful when it's recognized for what is currently is: a many-to-many communication methodology that allows greater access to information and resources in a way that allows efficiencies of transactions and knowledge transfer. Economics 101 mandates that somebody pay for that service. In that regard, the rules of competition will be the same as they are for bricks and mortar. The best services that add value to businesses and lives will thrive, while those that are discretionary or whimsical will falter.

Your eyes comprise a sensory organ. Eyes make somebody money when they are the recipients of cosmetics, shields, or surgery, or when they are used to appreciate a visual event. They don't make money when they watch for free. If you could sit in the bleachers and watch the game just as well as if you sat in a box seat at one thousand dollars a pop, which would you choose? The business failures of e-health have demonstrated that consumers have an insatiable appetite for medical information, but that they will not pay for that information. Medical content on the Internet has become a loss leader for businesses that are based on transactions. As such, it is like charity care, which receives less scrutiny than it should for quality.

PHYSICIAN HEAL THYSELF

Leadership has as much potential to bring out the worst in someone as to bring out the best. Doctors don't handle that sort of pressure any better than anyone else, as noted by their propensity for domestic divorce, suicide, and substance abuse. The formulae for leadership and stress are identical. What does the doctor tell you when stress leads to high blood pressure, headaches, and chest pain? Get rid of the stress. So, what is my advice when leadership is the cause of the stress? Well, if you can't quit your job, something has to change. Furthermore, doctors and executives often find themselves in leadership positions without having received any leadership training. Self-assessment should be high on your list of recurring activities. Listen carefully to what you are told and you'll find the advice in this section to be useful.

When You Circle the Wagons, Don't Shoot In

This is my favorite advice. When the Joint Commission on Accreditation of Hospitals rides into town, the wagons circle in a hurry. During one of the Joint Commission's hospital surveys, it's inevitable that something is found to be wrong. There are too many people being treated in the hall,

Paul S. Auerbach, M.D.

the medication cabinet isn't kept locked, the file room is inaccessible, the staff seem too happy, or there's some criticism the surveyors have cooked up to justify their existence. When a hospital is cited, it's at risk for bad publicity and losing patients, so everyone scrambles for cover. The first response in the hospital is to find someone to blame, to direct the wrath of hospital administration anywhere but at you. Doctors and nurses gather in "crisis meetings" and the finger pointing starts. Everyone turns on everyone else in an effort to find a scapegoat for the sins of the past.

When the settlers rode in wagon trains across the prairie, they sometimes came under attack. The classic line of defense was to circle the wagons, place the women and children in the center, arm the defenders on the periphery, and shoot out at the attackers. Who would ever think to shoot in?

Times will be tough, no doubt about it. And there will occasionally need to be disciplinary actions in the heat of battle. However, when strong-willed people who are normally smart and motivated turn against each other instead of against their real adversaries, then the battle will be lost, or if it is won, the number of casualties will be excessive. This is where true leadership can save the day. Internal recrimination at a time when everyone is looking to you for solutions and support usually results in instant demoralization, from which you may not be able to recover.

I have led groups of students through simulated resuscitations of a critically injured individual, who is prepared with makeup and instructed to deteriorate whether or not the students make the right moves. That is, the victim is supposed to get worse instead of better, sometimes against logic. In real life, these things happen. I want to see how the students work together and how they react to stress. The victim gets worse and worse, and by the end of the demonstration, dies.

Invariably, the group is initially stunned. During the activities, at least one person has gotten flustered and then angry, criticizing someone for the fact that the patient hasn't improved. It has to be somebody's fault, right? Usually the most vocal individual turns out to be someone who thinks he has personally screwed up. Perhaps he has, but many times he hasn't, just thinks he has. A person who has recently experienced the loss of a friend or family member, or has been involved in the death of a patient, may begin to weep. Afterwards, the militant student resents what I have just put him through, while the self-impressed student thinks the entire exercise is stupid, because the actor didn't mimic reality. They start to argue with each other about the meaning of what happened, and then they get personal. In trying to find someone to blame for what happened, they recognize each other's weaknesses. The truly insecure or mean-spirited need to find someone, anyone, to whom they can direct the blame. When it starts to get ugly, I jump in and point out how difficult it is for a team to hang together under such adverse circumstances.

How much responsibility does a manager have for the creation of internal conflict that emanates from an outside force? Quite a bit, if he doesn't guide the process. Let's say your company just moved to a new office and in the process, multiple systems needed to be replaced or upgraded. Transitions are hard. At a baseline, people are going to be inefficient and tired until they can settle into their new surroundings. The new phone system doesn't work well and your customers are frustrated at the lack of communication, the thermostat won't regulate and everyone in the office complains that they're freezing, and your new letterhead arrives with three misspellings and the logo printed backward. When you gather your operations staff and ask what the heck is going on, you can let them shift the blame and bark at each other, in which case it becomes *your* fault, or you can methodically assess all of your systems, empower a clean-up crew, put your shop in order, and hand out bonuses for all of the hard work that's been done.

If there's a big disaster, save the internal dirty work for well after you have done what it takes to get the problem solved. When the surveyors come and try to create the internal chaos upon which they can build their case for a reprimand, don't give in to such a simple tactic. If you have the presence of mind to circle the wagons, grab your rifles and point them out, not in.

Don't Take It Home with You

The E.R. is as unpredictable and intense an environment as exists in medicine. None of the patients wants to be there. The baseline emotions are pain, fear, and impatience. The patients who aren't very sick want to be treated and released in a hurry, and those that are quite ill are frightened and may even be dying. This isn't the ophthalmologist's office, where someone with a few wrinkles needs a lid lift. It's loud, it's fast, and it's exhausting.

Everybody assumes I work out to stay in shape, but it's really to let off steam before I go home and expect my family to understand how bad I got beat up that day in the E.R. I have to find a way to decompress, because it isn't fair to take it home with me. How can you expect a family to relate to the type of intensity that allows one to not only function, but to dominate and be the lead force, in the maelstrom of a busy E.R.? I need to wind down or face a family that ducks for cover when I walk through the door.

However, believe it or not, *now* I look forward to my clinical work as a respite from the pressures of my corporate job. Many of the medical decisions seem much more straightforward, and ungoverned by motives of dominance and profit. I'm tired after a day seeing patients, but much less so than after a day of worrying about shareholders, return on investment, and whether or not a company will be able to go public. When the pressures of the day have been great, the ride home isn't pleasant. However, if I can't make the transition to tranquility or at least attain an emotional truce, then I'm a bear, and it shows in the mirror that's my family.

There are lots of reasons to leave it at the office. Nobody at home can really help you, and there's no reason to expect that they should. I find that talking about work when it's depressing doesn't go over very well. Why should your wife and kids listen to you gripe? For that matter, why should anyone else? Even if you love your work, the time away should be refreshing, round you out as a person, and demonstrate that there's more to life than landing the deal. If you can participate in something that's satisfying, even if it's simple, it will make work seem that much more unique and something to look forward to, rather than dread. When you carry a bad mood, it's like coughing into a crowd. Nobody wants to be around you, and nobody wants your germs. The next time you walk in the door and growl at someone, imagine that you're throwing up in the middle of a movie theater. Everybody heads for the exit.

Stand Down

Anyone who watches television knows that the E.R. is the closest thing that medicine has to the wild, wild West. It's an in-your-face, here it comes ready-or-not type of place that doesn't allow for luxurious introspection. It's a nonscheduled environment of major medical crises interspersed with every imaginable presentation of medical or social distress. Each encounter requires resolution, so the E.R. is a decision-making environment. If you are a wishy-washy doctor and don't like to move things forward, it's not the place for you.

In a typical day, I can expect to have to make a minimum of a half-dozen "big" decisions, most of these rapidly under observation in a tense situation. It's a process fueled by adrenaline and tempered by experience. When the crises appear in swift succession, after each tough call, there's a millisecond of letdown, before I have to wade in and fire off the next decision. I'm used to being in charge, having people pay attention to me, and squelching superfluous commentary. It can be a rough way to do business, but there isn't always time for niceties.

The intensity of the situations I encounter in the E.R. has made me better and worse in my ability to deal with problems away from work. I'm pretty good at thinking on my feet, and having been desensitized to the fear of facing many life and death situations, I'm not easily frightened by a big crisis in the workplace. When a huge issue explodes in a business, how much worse could it be than having to jump-start a fibrillating heart or secure an airway through a mangled face? That's good, because I can hold my equilibrium when others are screaming and running around like headless chickens. But the ability to manage a crisis is not very useful, and in fact can be counterproductive, when I'm faced with a problem of lesser acuity at work or of any sort away from work. I'm so programmed to deal with the big stuff that I become intolerant toward issues that seem to be less important (to me), particularly when they come from my family. Furthermore, I can even become indecisive, if you can believe that, if the decision isn't big enough, or if I have too many choices or too much time to think.

Put me in front of a man gushing blood from a huge wound and I'm methodical and cool as a cucumber. Put me in front of my kids trying to decide whether to go for a bike ride or a hike, and I'm paralyzed. Worse yet, I may become annoyed because they think this decision is a big deal.

Consider your behavior carefully. Do you find yourself barking at your people because their questions are annoying, and you "have more important things to be concerned about?" Do you find yourself saying, "I don't care," to half the questions you are asked by your managers and employees? Do you truly believe that you are not supposed to sweat the small stuff? Well, if you're in charge, and someone asks your opinion, give it to him and don't act perturbed. Unless someone is pathologically dependent, indecisive, or sucking up, engaging you in the small stuff is their way of deriving feedback and support. Furthermore, what's not particularly important to you may be highly significant to them. When you are with other people, you don't have the option to tune out, unless you are willing to suffer the consequences of disaffection.

Chainsaws Are for Trees, Not People

A famous CEO achieved the moniker of "Chainsaw Al." I don't know whether or not he was proud of his nickname, but I hope not. *Chainsaws are for trees, not people.* I've personally cared for persons who were cut by chainsaws and it wasn't pretty.

A chainsaw approach has no place in business. Amputation is avoided unless one is forced to sever a limb that is irrevocably damaged. Removing a body part creates a deformity, which changes a person for life and creates physical and psychological handicaps regardless of how deftly it is performed.

The corporate chainsaw is applied as a brutal analogy for lopping off a failing business unit, for downsizing the company to control costs, or for laying off workers who no longer contribute to profits. It carries the logger's connotation of a rough cut, of chopping, of swiftness, and of finality. In this age of mergers and consolidations, what is the alternative?

I believe the alternatives are finesse and compassion, in recognition that severing a tree limb is not the same as performing plastic surgery on a mangled foot in order to save a human life. It's a pruning approach, as opposed to relentless harvest. And, it is sensitive to the recipient of the cutting, for whom nothing will ever again be the same.

An executive might lash out in a reflex to satisfy his shareholders by chopping off a failing business unit. The act may be necessary, but should it be done with glee and dispassion, or with sadness and great remorse? Investment bankers love strong leaders and do not as a general rule feel comfortable with executives who wear their hearts on their sleeves. But it should never be forgotten that they make money when the stock goes up and they make money when the stock goes down. In short, they live for the transaction. They are bankers and creators of wealth, but not necessarily contentment. An executive needs to satisfy the investment community, but has to live with the impact his decisions have on the lives of his employees. Style is important here. From time to time, we all have to let people go. Sometimes the cancer needs to be cut out. But nothing gets sliced before the alternatives are considered.

Never forget that the saw can kick back. The image of hot sharp metal ripping your trousers and zinging into your bones is indelible. Be thankful that the publisher wouldn't let me insert an illustration here. A chainsaw is a powerful weapon that requires two strong arms to maneuver and control. It cuts in a wide line and isn't designed for fine detail. In short, it's not a precision instrument. It's loud and obtrusive. Everyone knows when you are using it. It wakes them up.

What I'm trying to say is that I think "Chainsaw Al" would have been better off if he had been called "Miracle Al," "Unbelievable Al," or just plain "Al." He could have been just as tough, if he wished to be, and could have cultivated the image of a craftsman rather than a clear-cut forester. Wall Street was harsh with him because he didn't succeed, but I wonder if the people for whom he created opportunities are grateful, which in my mind is as least as important. For you readers who scoff and think that writing these words means I'm not tough or don't understand what it takes to run a business, you're wrong. Think about it the next time you're chopping wood. It doesn't take much of a slip to put the ax into your shin.

Reengineering Doesn't Come Easily to Anyone

Doctors are trained to practice medicine, not business. Even worse, they may not be trained in medical computing. What are the biggest reform issues in health care? The business of medicine and lack of data collection. Physicians are selected by most medical school admissions committees for their high grades, outstanding achievement in some specialized activity such as drama, and high test scores, none of which are predicated on a team approach to anything in particular. Med students are rugged individualists, chosen and then schooled in the best ways to respond to stressful situations where rapid judgments must be made and the rewards are mostly based upon outcomes linked to solo performance. Furthermore, the amount of information that must be learned and retained is immense. It's been stated that on the first day of medical school, a student is years behind and will almost certainly never catch up. One learns precious ways of doing things in medical school. Out in practice, there's no time to change behaviors or techniques, because such continuing education invades productivity, a situation worsened by declining reimbursement. Habit becomes dogma.

217

Paul S. Auerbach, M.D.

The champions for change in the health-care system have not been the providers. Instead, patients, administrators, and government officials have recognized the need to do certain things differently and have taken control of the nonclinical aspects of health care. This is not good, because it only reinforces the role of the doctor as a technician, without acknowledging the cultural aspects of medicine.

Is this fair? In part, I guess it is. Perhaps it isn't my fault that I wasn't taught to be able to perform a self-assessment and to change. But I struggle at a time when circumstances demand that I must. Compare a surgeon to a concert pianist. The musician possesses extraordinary talent and devotes prodigious efforts to practice. But once the concerto is learned, the notes don't change. A piano is a piano. One can look forward to playing the same instrument over and over, with the keys the same size and color, and always in the same place. Now, take a heart surgeon. He first had to learn how to drill and cut. That took ten years beyond medical school. A couple of years later, he needed to learn how to operate through a fiberoptic scope, then a few years later to use a laser, and probably in a few years will need to learn how to manipulate a robot. Grafts and appliances change every few years, and so do antibiotics, drugs to combat rejection of transplants, diagnostic modalities, and so on and so forth. The change comes hard, because the old stuff worked, maybe just not quite as well. Now pile on the economics, and the review committee that takes the great outcome for granted—they just care how much it costs. The changes are necessary, I suppose, but that doesn't make them less painful. We haven't even begun to talk about pride and the discounting of experience in preference for technology.

The transition can be radical and difficult to accept. How do you take a racehorse and turn it into a trail horse, following in line nose-to-tail, scolded and whipped for trying to follow a new path? Is this what we mean by reengineering?

I think the biggest problem with reengineering is that there isn't a preliminary understanding of the preceding engineering. In other words, to change a critical path and have anyone buy into the change, everyone needs to understand how things are being done prior to the change, so that there's a frame of reference. It's not enough to say, "This is all wrong, you've got to change." You have to make the investment in time to understand your starting point, so that everyone can be part of the process and understand the journey from beginning to end. History is very important.

It's a rare person that likes to change. Suffering folks like to be relieved of their pain, poor people would like to have more money, and cold explorers enjoy the warmth of a shelter, but most contented, fed, and housed individuals are doing just fine, thank you. Creatures of habit, we each tend to like to eat the same foods, watch the same shows, and ski the same slopes, because familiarity is safe and it's easy. Corporations are no different. Changing the way we do business is a laborious process that inevitably shows up somebody's flaws, so most people avoid it. Reengineering, which implies that something *really* isn't working right, implies changing assignments, moving staff around, and perhaps even layoffs. It's inherently resisted, unless championed by persons who make it their livelihood to come into a company for the purposes of analysis and change.

How do you create a culture of change? I think this can be accomplished by intentionally giving people assignments that are out of their area of expertise and comfort zone, and then supporting them with time and resources to be successful in these assignments. Each employee should be mandated to make a recommendation for change at least once a year, and those that are accepted should be rewarded. Education should be continuous. If you have to play the same instrument your entire life, learn new songs and change the tempo. Play in front of different audiences. Don't always do it for the money. Play at a benefit. The audiences are more appreciative, and just as critical.

Telling the Truth Isn't Always Easy

The application of this principle takes many forms in the medical profession. At the most basic level, a patient is entitled to be informed about his condition based upon a full explanation offered at a level he can comprehend. It's easy to talk over someone's head, even hoping that there might be a slight misconnect. This is often done, consciously or unconsciously, to perpetuate an intellectual gap or to maintain control. Personally, I think it's a lazy man's technique, because it takes more effort to organize one's thoughts in another person's frame of reference. However, in a situation where the transfer of information is critical, that obligation can be the crucial determinant in the nature of a relationship, particularly when the news isn't good. Doctors talk to each other in "medi-speak," which is abbreviated and often devoid of emotion. Persons are referred to as disease states ("Go see the heart attack up in the Unit"), there is a vernacular for unsavory or dead characters ("gomers" and "stiffs"), and the essential elements of communication are brevity and encryption. This is precisely the opposite of the approach that needs to be taken with patients.

It's OK to soften the blow if that helps get a patient through a crisis, or even to bend the truth when the situation is dismal and calls for a dose of hope. There are ethical boundaries that should not be crossed involved with manipulation of the facts undertaken for the benefit of a patient. But these are rare circumstances. A physician is often better prepared for a major event than for the day-to-day interchange that forms the bulk of his reporting obligation.

I dread sitting down with young parents and telling them that their child has died. Nearly every resuscitation for a victim of cardiac arrest ends with a personal

Paul S. Auerbach, M.D.

tragedy for someone. The family dog bites off a lip and someone has to tell mom that her daughter will need a skin graft that will leave a scar for life. Your father has Alzheimer's disease and is never going to be able to feed himself. You have a lump in your breast.

Whew! These are tough communications that require time and compassion. While I'm wrestling with my own emotions, often projecting the horror and sadness onto myself as I imagine that the misery is directed at my own family, I must somehow pay attention to how my message is being received. How well are they listening? When do I back off and let them grieve? If they are in disbelief, do I restate the facts, give them a hug, or walk away and say I'll be back in a few minutes? What if they don't speak English? You see, telling the truth isn't easy or ever enough. I have to feel the truth and experience it while I pass it along, so that I can anticipate and react in a way that will get the message across and provide support through a difficult situation.

People ask me how I deal with the intense emotional roller coaster generated in the E.R. Private tears are the answer. Not because I am afraid to show myself to a patient, but because my staff needs to appreciate my stability. They know how we all suffer at times, but there is value in a professional approach from a leader. It's a personal choice that works for me.

Short of telling someone that they are about to be fired or that the company is about to go bankrupt, it's a little easier in the corporate suite. The worst news you have to deliver is that someone isn't doing a good job or working hard enough. Furthermore, everyone basically speaks the same language, although there is still the potential for misunderstanding when someone lapses into technical jargon. It's critically important to establish that people should speak up if they require an explanation or clarification. It serves no purpose for someone to sit in silence and ignorance out of fear of embarrassment. This occurs when the general climate imposes criticism and judgment rather than education and support.

Lest this sound too squishy, let me say that I'm not advocating a group therapy session when the issues at hand are performance and expectations. It's appropriate and necessary for a senior manager to express displeasure when there have been inadequacies and underachievement. However, the fact-gathering phase should be calm and dispassionate, and the punishment should fit the crime. That the medium is often the message must never be lost on an executive, who is under the constant scrutiny of his employees.

To be an effective communicator, you must get everyone speaking the same language at the same level and operating with the intention of achieving understanding, rather than creating a smokescreen, unless this is your specific intention. Negotiation is a separate issue that might be excluded from these admonitions.

Paul S. Auerbach, M.D.

Learn on the Job before You
Call in the Consultants

A cynic proclaims that the difference between a consultant and a Boy Scout is that the scout has adult supervision. There are, of course, valid reasons to outsource your
creative thinking, but not as many as you might think. If
you need to garner true expertise or don't have the time
to complete a critical project, then a good consultant can
be a lifesaver. However, if using consultants becomes
regular, then you will limp along.

Why do emergency physicians call consultants to
assist them with patients? Here are the reasons:

- The patient needs a specialist's attention. An
  example would be a heart attack victim who
  needs to go to the catheterization laboratory
  for an angioplasty or a victim with a disfigur-
  ing laceration who requires the skill of a plastic surgeon. This is a good reason.

- The E.R. is extremely busy and additional
  hands are needed to decompress the clinical
  area. If the waiting time for patients has
  grown too long, the extra doctor can help
  move people through. This is a good reason.

- The consultant has a responsibility to come to
  the E.R. as part of a protocol, or team. For
  instance, there is often a trauma team that is
  paged to respond when a victim with a certain
  level or mechanism of injury appears. This is a
  good reason.

- A "celebrity" appears as a patient. It can be a true celebrity, like a movie star, or it can be a political celebrity, like the child of a hospital trustee, who is likely to tell all and complain about the wait for service. In some respects, the use of a consultant invokes a double standard. Aren't the rest of the patients just as important? This is a marginal reason.

- The emergency physician wants a second opinion, either because he isn't sure of a diagnosis or because he doesn't want to accept the medical-legal risk on his own. This can be good or bad, depending on who pays the bill and how much it inconveniences the patient. It's good if useful new information is acquired and bad when it's just passing the buck.

The above examples demonstrate that a consultant can fit many different definitions for the purpose of accomplishing a wide variety of tasks, but in only a single medical scenario (the first) is the act of consultation perhaps an act of creativity. More often than not, it's an act of manpower, the reinforcement necessary to keep the process moving in a direction articulated by the true leader. So, what is creativity in the E.R.? It's the amalgamation of history and physical findings that leads the clinician to determine a diagnosis. Then, unless there's a straightforward therapeutic path, it's the integration of medicines, splints, stitches, bandages, social services, psychological counseling, crisis intervention, and all the other assorted pieces necessary to shift the patient from the zone of maximal discomfort to a process of healing. This must be accomplished between a doctor and a patient that typically have no preexisting relationship. What advantage does a consultant have here?

It's manpower again, unless you have reached a creative impasse or are too fatigued to muster your imagination. Sometimes it just helps to have someone share the load, and a consultant serves as a confidant. Other times, one can actually get an onerous process delegated away, and then approach other tasks that are more manageable or appealing.

It's fascinating to watch how consultants are used in medicine, depending upon the payment mechanism. In a fee-for-service environment, consultants are used a lot, and the charge is back to the insurance company or patient. In a managed care environment, where all of the care rendered has to be paid for out of a predetermined dollar amount, the use of consultants plummets, because it cuts into somebody's profit.

In the executive suite, the use of consultants is seen as both strength and a weakness. The important consideration is to know how to manage your consultants. When someone asks me what I learned in business school, I answer, "I learned how to use my consultants." In a one-year executive program, it was impossible to become a world-class accountant, financial analyst, marketer, or strategic planner. I was exposed to experts in these areas, and observed the quality of process and performance that culminated in outstanding work. This has become invaluable in my ascent as a manager and advisor. While I might have migrated to a specific area of expertise, I of necessity become a generalist. I frequently need to rely upon the work of others. I assume that all of my employees are actually consultants to me and so I must gauge the quality of their work. You can only hold people to high standards if you can recognize high standards, and therein lies the true value of a business education. You will become adept at what you practice; the rest you must recognize and judge, and accept or reject.

Go Top Down or Bottom Up, but Remember That Your Customers Pay for the Service

It's amazing to me that many physicians are intimidated by the customer service concept. This probably stems from a traditional interpretation of the doctor-patient relationship. While the doctor serves the patient, it's the role of the patient to accept the wisdom of the physicians without criticism, in deference to their superior knowledge and the assumption that a doctor will automatically be able to do what's in the best interest of a patient.

Times have changed. Health care has been recognized as an expensive commodity with many interchangeable parts, including the men and women who call themselves doctors. The customer pays the bills, and increasingly calls the shots. Obtaining a second opinion is small stuff compared to authorizations, concurrent review, quality assurance programs, and retrospective audits. Employers recognize that their single largest cost after manufacturing is health care, and they are not pleased. We can adopt whatever management style we like in health care, driven top down by the health plans and hospitals, or bottom up by the physicians and nurses, but the bottom line is that it will ultimately be the patients or their advocates that determine which of us get to practice medicine and how and where we will be allowed to do that. In the final reckoning, I would not be surprised to see America evolve to a national health program, but this will have grave implications for consumer choice, so perhaps it won't be a reality until an aging population, technology, and new drugs bankrupt the health-care entitlement programs.

Excessive costs are being squeezed out of the system pretty quickly, so the next parameters of performance will be related to outcomes and satisfaction. Since there is no comprehensive national database upon which to compare outcomes, satisfaction and other subjective measures of the health-care experience are at the top of everyone's agenda.

Sound familiar? Do you have difficulty measuring what you believe is important in your business? Is your customer focused on an entirely different agenda when you determine how to measure satisfaction? When was the last time you asked a customer what was really important, and then acted on the response?

Your customers call the shots. Requests for service may know no boundaries, but within your definition of a management services agreement, you need to deliver. Beating financial projections will make you popular with the analysts, but beating expectations with your customers will keep you sane. Customer loyalty is derived from a great number of intangibles, which makes the dialogue between you and your customers even more important. If you are initiating a new customer, understand that customer. Don't play pin the tail on the donkey.

When a patient is hooked to a blood pressure monitor, I can look at the numbers and know where I am. When a patient has pain, the evaluation is subjective, and I must use my understanding of the process to determine whether I am making any headway. While you may have a captive customer through a particular episode, if you haven't met his needs, you won't have the opportunity to serve him again.

Be Moral

Morality is manifest in many different ways, but in the business world, it usually relates to money. Said differently, managers lose their judgment when they aren't going to make their numbers. The two biggest symptoms of a pending financial morality lapse are overexaggerating your capabilities and cutting corners. Unfortunately, you can't save your way to heaven. Great managers

Paul S. Auerbach, M.D.

operate "within themselves," understand their short-comings, continually try to improve, and structure their continuing education to meet the needs of their customers. Their self-improvement is a service ethic, not an exercise in self-aggrandizement.

A doctor treats a patient with a forehead laceration. The wound is only four inches long, but the record reflects that six inches were closed. If the intent was to collect more money, that's fraud. Is it worth it? I guess it depends on whether you believe the power of money is worth the potential loss of license, reputation, and career, not to mention violation of the doctor-client relationship. Should doctors be held to a higher standard? I think so.

A manager has informed Wall Street repeatedly that the quarter's numbers will come in close to estimates, but he knows that there isn't a snowball's chance in the desert. Some fancy accounting can shift a few expenses and book a little extra revenue, but technically, that's fraud. Is it worth it? I guess it depends on whether you believe that keeping your stock price artificially inflated is worth the loss of reputation, wrath of the Board, or even a stint behind bars. Should managers be held to a higher standard? I think so.

There is no justifiable excuse for any breach of moral obligation, in medicine or in business. Cutting corners while boasting of achievement is the fastest entry to the slippery slope of deception deployed to cover the previous swindle. I'm not referring to weaknesses like drug abuse, which render a person ineffective, because in the end, these are personal tragedies that become totally consumptive. Rather, I'm concerned with the flawed behaviors that are perpetrated to unfairly accumulate wealth, of the violation of principles and trust that are resident in a moral framework. The ultimate workplace disruption is a breach of integrity that becomes public knowledge. When this happens, one may be able to continue to lead by intimidation, but the respect is gone and with it, the intense loyalty that becomes necessary during a corporate crisis.

Pity Others before Yourself

I've listened to physicians moan and groan about managed care, and business people whine about investment bankers. Having to manage patients within budgets has completely altered the landscape of medicine and changed the expectations of income and lifestyle for many physicians. Whether or not you agree with the tenets of managed care, it's here to stay in one form or another.

Woe is me? Perhaps, but that won't get me very far. Doctors are not well trained to change. Some would argue that they are trained to *not* change. They learn a certain set of drugs, learn certain operative techniques, and are inundated with medical knowledge to the extent that by the time a young doctor graduates from medical school, he or she is in a state of sensory overload. When you are one hundred thousand-plus dollars in debt, have been in school for twenty years, trained for another five years to become a specialist and need to establish roots before your spouse leaves you for someone who comes home from time to time, that's not precisely when you want to hear that you can look forward to longer hours, less money, more bureaucracy, and zero adulation.

So, do you wallow in self-pity and hold out until all of your patients belong to another network and you can't earn enough to cover the office overhead? Do you badmouth the bureaucrats, blame everything on government intervention, shut down your practice, and abandon your lifelong dream? Hell, no! You retrain, retool, figure out what everyone else seems to have learned, and *change*. If you can't learn how to adapt, then the next generation of doctors, who will be indoctrinated with philosophies and habits that you aren't willing to adopt, will be delighted to take care of your patients.

I've listened to physicians state that they resent having their patients referred to as "customers." This is somehow supposed to be demeaning. I think it's an improvement. We're finally facing the fact that patients have choices, and that there's a dominant element of service in the delivery of medicine that cannot be ignored. This does not in any way mitigate the respect that should be accorded to the medical profession for the intensity of its training, work ethic, and responsibility. However, the fact is that there may be too many doctors, and no one doctor has a lock on the market.

Doctors love to complain about their hours, particularly during training. Well, no one ever said it would be easy. While it's foolish and potentially dangerous to have medical trainees work to exhaustion, there's too much to learn and not enough time in which to learn it. No one has a God-given right to become a doctor. You go into it understanding that there will be sacrifices. If you want to make them, then you become a physician and look forward to a meaningful professional career for life. If you don't want to make them, then sell software.

In the executive suite, it can be stressful and isolated. Suppliers demand more favorable terms, employees want raises, the stock market trashes your sector, and the Board of Directors wants results—now! Multi-tasking your way through the terrain of top management, it's tempting to ponder why this appears so dehumanizing. When you're feeling sorry for yourself, take a step back and determine if the situation is unfair, or whether you are just tired. A "mental health day" is often all that's necessary to get you out of a funk. However, no matter what the solution to your current problems, don't lapse into feeling sorry for yourself, because you *don't have to be there.* I mean, you truly do not need to be there, physically or emotionally. You are being well compensated to do a high-level job which you theoretically desire. If you are beginning to resent what the life-style or job requirement is doing to your psyche, take a break or make a switch. Feeling sorry for yourself only bleeds into your relationships at work and at home, and makes people want to distance themselves from you. Who wants to be around a sad sack?

I'm not arguing against making job demands reasonable, or promoting a healthy approach to work and the balance between your office and the rest of the world. What I am saying is that all talented people have choices. A person who knows how to budget his time and get his work done can almost always define the parameters of how the job is structured. This certainly should be true for executives, and is increasingly true for physicians.

Snakes Don't Read Books

I remember a young boy who was brought in for treatment after having been bitten by a rattlesnake. When I asked him what happened, he said that he was walking in the woods when a rattlesnake shot up from the ground and bit him on the leg. The boy was tearful and indignant. "The snake didn't rattle. I didn't hear anything. We learned about snakes in school and they're supposed to rattle before they strike. It isn't fair."

All I could think to tell him was something I had heard many years before from a rattlesnake expert. "Son, snakes don't read books."

Bad things happen, and good things happen. Either way, it's rarely according to plan and often not anything like the way it's supposed to be. A rattlesnake is supposed to shake its rattle when it's threatened, warning the potential predator to watch out. However, you can come on a snake too quickly for it to have a chance to rattle, or the rattle may be inactive because of a molt, or the snake may just not feel like it. If you are bitten, you lose.

It's essential to know how to go by the book, but even more essential to know how to react and to improvise. Resuscitating a victim of major trauma highlights the need to assess, react, and then reassess. The single most difficult habit to ingrain in a young physician is the importance of reevaluation, of never accepting the status quo. If the book says that a patient won't drop his blood pressure until he loses thirty percent of his blood volume, it's no guarantee that this won't occur with much lower blood loss. Although the classic presentation of a heart attack is pain in the center of the chest with radiation into the jaw and left arm, the emergency physician soon discovers that a heart attack can occur with pain in the right shoulder or with no pain at all. The most potent anti-inflammatory steroid drug used to treat an allergic reaction can cause a severe allergic reaction itself!

I've walked into a meeting with a major supplier to discover that it was on the verge of bankruptcy, and that a critical service upon which my business was totally dependent was about to be curtailed. Without a contingency plan, the fallout of this event would have been to severely impact our ability to serve our clients, and likely the loss of significant customers. We didn't have adequate backup, because our supplier was supposed to be infallible. The work involved to resurrect our supply chain was tenfold that if we had been adequately prepared. This was a lesson that I wouldn't care to repeat.

The Best Doctors Have Been Patients

Empathy is an extremely powerful force in medicine, and should be equally powerful in business. In order to understand how best to care for, in the truest sense of caring, their patients, it's essential that physicians spend time as patients or acting in the roles of patients. This exercise can also be completed by being the parent of an ill relative, in a situation where one becomes truly vulnerable to the system and ministrations of the health-care providers. It's a humbling experience, as one realizes how truly dependent the average person is in the overwhelming experience of illness. Position yourself as a patient, and you become weak, tired, in pain, frightened, anxious, depressed, and in search of hope, relief, and an end to suffering. Imagine losing a loved one, and what is truly important in your life. Think then about the faith one puts in a physician and how desperately one needs to be heard, understood, and supported. Doctors who have an inadequate bedside manner may have never been ill or forced to deal with the illness of someone close to them.

A patient needs to know that his physician "has been there," can appreciate his suffering, and is motivated to find a cure as quickly as possible. A doctor must establish trust, both to motivate the patient and to facilitate communication when the situation becomes complex. One genuine and effective way to do this is to show empathy, not in a gratuitous manner, but with feeling and conviction. If you are caring for a patient the same way you would care for a family member, there's nothing wrong in letting the patient know. Within the boundaries of maintaining appropriate leadership and autonomy, personalizing the relationship is a strongly positive technique that encourages the patient to view the doctor as empathetic. There's nothing wrong with revealing to a patient that you as a physician have been in a similar situation, and understand your patient's concerns from a very personal perspective. That gives your patient some confidence that he's being treated as a human being with real needs, rather than as a statistic or an organism dispassionately analyzed for its particular pathophysiology. A mother or father with a sick child might like to know that you have children. We all have parents who grow old and infirm.

Whenever possible, put yourself in the other person's shoes. How soon would you want to be seen? How quickly would you like to be called back? How much of an explanation would you require? Would you like to hear about alternatives to therapy, or to the percentage of chances for success? Would you want a second opinion? Would you like to have your hand held, or a cool cloth placed against your forehead? What are your greatest fears and how soon should they be addressed? If you can truly appreciate the needs of those you serve and for whom you are responsible, then you cannot help but provide better service.

Furthermore, transfer this approach to the young physicians-in-training for whom you have supervisory responsibility. What are their pressures? What help do they need? How well you can serve as a mentor and role model may depend on how well you can reminisce about when you were at that stage, and how you would have preferred to be treated.

I have been a patient in the E.R. and, flat on my back on a stretcher, "looked up at the lights." I have agonized over the health of my children and prayed for compassion and wisdom in the doctors who have cared for them. As best I can, I force myself to think back to these situations long enough to appreciate how I can create an emotional, or at least functional, communication link to my patient. If my goal is to relieve suffering or at least to provide guidance, I need to offer what the patient truly needs, not what I want them to need or think they should need. This does not negate my ability to have an opinion or responsibility to tell the truth, but rather, reinforces these functions.

Perhaps less is at stake in the corporate suite, but this would only be in terms of life and death. The people's needs are the same. There are many difficult situations expressed in terms of market share, profit and loss, quarterly earnings, and public market expectations. Failure may not cost you a limb in the literal sense, but what about self-esteem, a critical promotion, or your professional reputation? These are critical issues that require a manager to address how best to empathize with employees, consultants, shareholders, and customers.

How practical is this? It becomes more and more difficult the higher one rises in the administration of a company, which often necessitates a more broad-brush approach and delegation to lower level managers. The error here would be to populate the organization chart below or around you with nonempathetic individuals who cannot serve as surrogates for you in the critical relationships. If the hard-hearted among you can neither empathize nor staff with empathetic individuals, you are generating a situation destined for failure. This is not bleeding-heart liberalism, but practical advice for managers who believe that how they manage people says a great deal about how they will manage their business.

When someone is doing poorly, ask yourself what help is necessary to achieve a turnaround, and determine if it should be provided. If the answer is yes, then do what you can. If it is no, then put yourself in the failing position and ask, "Would I give up?" If it is important enough to provide something and you can provide it, then consider doing that, unless your strategy leads you to determine that natural selection is the best path. I can vouch from personal experience that the empathetic approach is more laborious, but when it works, much more satisfying than an arm's length solution.

Paul S. Auerbach, M.D.

The Technologic Imperative

The technologic imperative is the force that drives one to use a highly technical, and commonly expensive, solution for a problem when a more simple solution might suffice. An example in medicine would be to order an unnecessary and costly test, when the diagnosis is already fairly well nailed down. You don't have to use the equipment just because it is there. You should use what you need to use for very good reasons. The challenge of technology is to understand it well enough to be able to deploy it sensibly. I will never argue that you can have too much information, but you can certainly have redundant or unnecessary information.

There will always be improvements. Look at what has occurred with digital cameras in the past two years. At what point are you sufficiently satisfied with the quality of what is available and do you make the purchase? Consider the Internet. Do you invest in an Internet strategy now or do you wait for others to show you the path? I think it depends on the nature of your business relationships. If your trading partners expect to communicate with you via the Internet, you must find a current solution. Otherwise, you can afford to be patient, because with each passing day, the solutions are less complex, easier to implement, and less expensive.

If your business is significant, you should have a Technology Officer. In health care, the Chief Information Officer (CIO) jobs have been fraught with frustration, because the charge was not just to opine on servers and networks, but to engage physicians to use computers in the practice of medicine. Good luck. Implementation of behavioral changes is very much different than deciding whether to install cable or wireless solutions. For the politics of technology, you must have the support of thought leaders. This is true for generic technology (such as information systems) as well as for specialty technology (such as heart catheters). Administratively driven technology solutions in health care have not been well received unless they were clearly championed by the providers, who take their advice from other providers—the more well-known and trusted, the better.

The TO in your company should be thoroughly familiar with how you do business and absolutely must have your complete support to implement essential technologies. I recommend that the first few implementations not represent big process changes. Let everyone get used to using new equipment, which is difficult enough, before they are expected to adapt to new methods. The technologic imperative will always exist, and so needs to be managed carefully.

Acts of Compassion Are Simple and Direct

If you have paid attention to the pages that precede this one, you will have noticed the theme of compassion many times. That is because applying compassion is every bit as much a learned skill as stopping a nosebleed or diagnosing a heart attack.

Compassion in the medical setting is a combination of empathy, mercy, forgiveness, and kindness. It is a complex emotion that can almost seem out of place in the frantic activity of an emergency, with rapid decisions borne of life-and-death situations. Many times, it is an afterthought, applied to the family after a loved one has been lost, or when the realization occurs that something horrible has happened or is about to happen. That is not misplaced, but reactive. It's more effective to be compassionate prospectively, interweaving a truly caring attitude into the very fabric of ministering to a patient. This is not inconsistent with a critical care setting, but in fact, may be the only aspect that maintains an element of humanity in an otherwise dehumanizing situation.

From the patient's perspective, the act of compassion has to be simple and direct. It is not intended to make the medical outcome any better, but rather, to assist the patient through a difficult and frightening situation with the confidence that there is an element of caring present. It does not derive its strength from technical expertise, but from a connection with the patient that evokes a common understanding.

A simple example of compassion was when your mother held your forehead as you puked in the toilet, then washed your face. You would have survived without that assistance, but she showed that she cared, which was the most important thing that anyone could do for you. When I have a frightened patient, I try to find a connection, a simple statement or act that demonstrates that I understand the suffering, and that I am therefore completely devoted to its obliteration.

So it is with your business. I am always amazed to what degree some people will go to hide the fact that they are in pain. Struggling with an assignment, a client service representative avoids me in meetings, even avoids eye contact. I know that something is wrong, that he is failing or has failed. Does he think that I haven't been there before, that I haven't ever suffered as he is suffering? It isn't a big deal, but his ego gets in the way. He wants to impress me, to be stoic, to forego assistance. I want to touch him in a way so that he learns two things: that I understand our business and that it is my job to help him. The offer is made in private and in confidence. Why don't you let me help you with that? I've been there before and I know how to help you succeed. After we are finished, the credit will all be yours.

Another less pleasant form of compassion is a timely "resignation." Sometimes a person will fail, and there isn't anything you can do to pull him through. The puff-out-your-chest routine is to fire him. However, letting someone save face is never a bad idea, even among sworn enemies. So, by extending an olive branch, you terminate an unsuccessful relationship without eliminating a well-trodden and essential path to future opportunities and perhaps even friendship.

Paul S. Auerbach, M.D.

The Race to the Starting Line

We live our lives and build our businesses in order to cross the finish lines. Life is not a race, and neither is a business. There are milestones, to be sure, but the process should be viewed as perpetual, unless one is in it for the quick hit. We have learned again recently and emphatically that a liquidity event can mean the acquisition of great wealth or the liquefaction of a flimsy business experiment.

Sequencing the human genome has been likened to a race to the starting line. I like that analogy and love the idea that there is now so much more to learn that no person can expect to plumb the depths of this new knowledge in a single lifetime. Think of all the wonderful associations with beginnings: birth, new, young, creation, growth, design, foundation, growth, discovery, etc. Now think about endings: death, final, termination, demolition, old, failure, involution.

If You Have Long-Term Goals,
You Need Long-Term Solutions

Physical rehabilitation is rarely a rapid process. A person who suffers a ski accident and loses the integrity of her knee ligaments can look forward to surgery, a few weeks of crutch walking, and then an arduous program of strengthening exercises and gradual return to normal activity. The surgery takes a couple of hours, while the recovery can be expected to last for months. Without a good program for therapy and a knowledgeable therapist to coach the patient and measure her progress, the ultimate outcome can be suboptimal and culminate in long-term disability. The goal is total recovery, supported by surgery, rehabilitation, and modification of future athletic activities. The surgery alone rarely suffices as a satisfactory solution. The patient must show patience and cooperate with the plan, even if there are minor setbacks. Reevaluation of the fundamental premise is undertaken if results don't match expectations or if there are complications.

If you want to build market share by, say, building a new type of sales force or changing the image of your company, it's difficult to have that happen overnight. There's almost always resistance, even if it's subtle, to change and start new programs. A rapid change in marketing strategy, new logo, spicy advertisement, or even acquisition to penetrate a market segment provides a jump-start, just like the surgeon reattaching ligaments. However, the follow-through determines the success or failure of your new efforts. Where do you want to be in six months, one year, and three years? What infrastructure has to be created and supported as you reach your milestones? Where are the correction points, and who will be entrusted with the evaluations? Are you capitalized to carry your efforts over the long haul? Are the expectations of the team the same as the expectations of senior management? Do you have a plan or is this an exercise in improvisation? In the E.R., we are always reacting, guessing (yes, guessing), trying to surround an acute problem with as broad a differential diagnosis as possible and then homing in on the likely suspects. As much as I hate to admit it, we are often more reactive than proactive, seeking more "not to miss something" than to be precise and cost effective. That's because the E.R. presents a patient who is often unknown to the doctor, without a relevant medical record, and in a hurry to achieve some measure of relief. Long-term care plans require contemplation and follow-up. In a business, while you will certainly need to throw a few stitches and set a few bones, you should strive to be organized and orderly, avoiding an acute-care mentality and therefore framing your activities with a long-term perspective.

Put a Picture of Your Family on Your Desk

This is a reminder to keep things in perspective and to always treat others as if they were members of your family. In trying to work your way through a difficult problem, draw upon common experiences and analogies that can be understood by everyone involved.

There are many situations in medicine where tough decisions have to be made, either to treat or to withhold treatment. Emotions can run high, particularly in the E.R. What the physician perceives as hostility and mistrust on the part of a patient or his family is actually just a venting of anxiety, sadness, or helplessness. A communication that comes off as a lecture or is perceived as too one-sided when the decision-making process needs to be shared saps precious energy from the task at hand, which should be to direct everyone's attention to improving the condition of the victim.

Before I talk to a patient or family member, I always imagine what style of communication I would prefer, if I were to be in a similar situation. It would be direct and logical, with some indication that the physician appreciated my suffering and was concerned with a prompt resolution. I would expect to have time for explanation of difficult concepts, and be allowed to ask as many questions as needed to allow me to be informed about my condition and the ramifications of any decisions. I would like to have choices, if there were any, and I would like everything explained at the level of my understanding. I would want to be treated like family.

Despite a good approach to communication, the respondents can be too indecisive for the impatient physician, who needs to have decisions made in a timely fashion, for the benefit of the patient, and to benefit his time management. It is of legitimate concern that there are other patients to see and that a physician's time is valuable. Unless a bona-fide second opinion is necessary, if I find a mother questioning whether or not her child should be placed on antibiotics or whether the cut really requires stitches, I tell her that I am a parent, and that this is how I would treat my own child. This simple expression is not a cheap trick to achieve her approval. Rather, it is a reminder to me of how important it is to remember that I at times will be the recipient of similar advice, and allows me to express my concern for her child at a level even more sacred than that of a physician.

When my struggling sales manager sits before me, heart racing and pupils dilated, and cowers in anticipation of a dreaded reprimand, all that good adrenaline is getting wasted on the "flight or fight" reaction. He should have learned long before that I wouldn't squander his time or my time on recrimination. A mature child should be able to come to a parent (mentor) and expect a firm hand and problem solving. Love and respect do not mean accepting all sorts of substandard behavior, but rather, setting a good example, communicating clearly, and allowing persons to make a few mistakes as they achieve their own form of excellence. The photo of my family reminds me that the same way that I would allow my children the benefit of the doubt, knowing full well when they are trying and when they are dogging it, so must I support my employees.

Finally, a regular glance at family and friends helps keep everything in perspective. How many times have you heard someone say, "My work is important, but my family comes first." It's hard to argue with that, but maybe a better thought would be, "My work and my family are both important. I keep them in balance and try to learn from them each day, so that I can have the best of both worlds."

Remember Why and How You Became a Doctor

The most difficult part of any job is keeping it interesting. There are many reasons why people become doctors, but the single common theme is a willingness and desire to learn, intensively at first and sporadically for the rest of their lives. If any of us look back at our medical careers and try to select the moments that were of greatest satisfaction, each is associated with an experience in which we learned something or applied our special knowledge in a way that was beneficial to someone in distress. Most emergency physicians love the challenge of thinking on their feet, and accept the responsibilities that come with the stress of having to make quick decisions in critical situations. They become less effective when they cannot continue to learn at a pace sufficient to keep up with modern medicine, or when they spend too many hours in the trenches and begin to burn out. Finally, if for some reason they are no longer inquisitive, they become bored, which is the kiss of death.

Persons in senior management can neither hug the status quo nor be afraid to grow and encourage others to do the same. Maintenance mode is reactive and defensive, not something that leads an individual or company to greatness. I became a doctor to learn and to help people. When I found myself in a position that defied intensive learning, I went to graduate school in business. I have held senior management positions in corporations, which presented continuous opportunities to learn and apply new knowledge. Now, I am continuing to practice medicine and helping startups. What is the common theme? Exploration. Something new. I need to be where it is happening, not where it's already happened. I recognize that I'm a knowledge junkie, and am willing to make occupational adjustments in pursuit of activities that are stimulating and on the cutting edge.

If you became a doctor to help people, then don't let the restrictions of managed care come between you and your patients. If you became a CEO to introduce a new paradigm of telecommunications, don't let a competitor bully you into submission. If you became a doctor to find a cure for cancer, lobby for research dollars until you no longer have the strength to raise your voice. If you became a marketing executive because you were tired of the drivel broadcast over television to children, reach into their minds and teach them why it is important to study and help their fellow man. If you became a doctor to give something back to the community, serve your patients with compassion and be their advocates when others would ration their ability to seek novel treatments for incurable diseases. If you became a Wall Street analyst to enable people to make intelligent investments with their hard-earned money, learn the truth and deliver it straight up.

It's good to have your heroes and to emulate great people that have gone before you. A small child pretends to win the Olympics, and we smile in amusement. Well, she believes that she could be the best in the world. If *you* don't, then *she* should be the CEO, not you.

Your business is important, maybe more so to others than it is to you. If you're in charge, it's your responsibility to nurture and protect it. To be less than fully devoted is to be disrespectful to those who do not carry your authority and therefore don't have the same opportunity to have a positive impact.

When I walk into a room and somebody asks for my help, I'm reminded why I became a doctor. I still love it.

Index